Also by Louis Auchincloss

Fiction

Nonfiction

The Style's the Man

Reflections on Proust, Fitzgerald, Wharton, Vidal, and Others

LOUIS AUCHINCLOSS

CHARLES SCRIBNER'S SONS

NEW YORK   LONDON   TORONTO   SYDNEY   TOKYO   SINGAPORE

CHARLES SCRIBNER'S SONS
Rockefeller Center
1230 Avenue of the Americas
New York, New York 10020

Manufactured in the United States of America

1   3   5   7   9   10   8   6   4   2

Library of Congress Cataloging-in-Publication Data
Auchincloss, Louis.
The style's the man: reflections on Proust, Fitzgerald,
Wharton, Vidal, and others / Louis Auchincloss.
p. cm.
A collection of essays, some previously published in the New York times book
review and the New York review of books.
ISBN 0-684-19742-1
1. Books—Reviews. 2. Literature—History and criticism.
I. Title. II. Title: Style's the man.
809—dc20   93-49792

For Diana and Alexander Hood

Le style est l'homme même.

—BUFFON

Contents

The Style's the Man

The Wit of
Ivy Compton-Burnett

❧

Joyce Carol Oates, reviewing Hilary Spurling's biography of Dame Ivy Compton-Burnett, speaks of the latter as a vogue that has passed and of "her use of puppet characters in sketchily realized settings" as suggesting an imaginative deficiency. Nathalie Sarraute, on the other hand, proclaims Dame Ivy as one of the most important novelists of our century and the leader in England of the *nouveau roman*.

So sharp a difference of opinion between two of the most perceptive critics of modern literature must send us in search of our own answer. After a careful rereading of Dame Ivy's twenty novels, I come down on the side of Sarraute. I am afraid that Oates, in finding naught in a Compton-Burnett novel but "a nineteenth-century closet drama that excludes all political and social verisimilitude," is looking only to the bare outward form of Dame Ivy's fiction.

What, then, is the substance? The substance to me is simply a new vision of human hearts and minds, deduced from the words that the characters exchange or sometimes merely whisper, words that are hammered into rhythmical sentences worthy of Congreve and Oscar Wilde. One of her characters says, "Words are all we have," to which another replies, "They are used as if they had some power. And how little they have!" That might be Dame Ivy's credo, as it might have been Congreve's and Wilde's. Words, words of little power, are all we have, but what beautiful things we can make of them! They are better than nothing.

It is constantly pointed out that Dame Ivy writes about English upper- or upper-middle-class country life in the late Victorian era. But this is only because she felt the need to anchor her plots to something. The vague outlines of houses, schools, and villages are depicted against a kind of backdrop, not really even intended to create an illusion, but simply to provide a setting other than bare walls, like the cardboard façades of castles or forts one might see in the window of a pet shop before which the puppies, hamsters, or rabbits are playing.

Nor are the plots much more convincing. Violent crimes, incest, and adultery make their almost casual appearance, to be greeted with faint surprise and little or no retribution. Josephine Napier in *More Women Than Men* picks up the unconscious body of her daughter-in-law and exposes it to a fatal chill from an open window. Hereward Egerton, in *A God and His Gifts*, seduces his son's fiancée, adopts the resulting child, and then persuades the son, ignorant of his father's role in the affair, to forgive and marry the girl. Yet Hereward subsequently gives himself away in the presence of his whole family by a monologue induced by his fond contemplation of the baby:

"The last, the child of my old age," said Hereward, almost to himself. "No other has been so much blood of my blood, so deeply derived from me."

Now why did Dame Ivy permit herself so clumsy a scene? I think she felt that everything had already been done that could be done in the English novel and that, seeking new ways of depicting human beings, she had to place her dialogue, consisting largely of subconversations, against a backdrop that would give them a frame without distracting from the main point, which was to reevaluate the human species. Her frames might be almost parodies of the standard nineteenth-century Victorian plot, with its murders, seductions, disappearances, and destroyed wills. The very names of her characters show her lifelong absorption in English fiction and history: Ponsonby, Swift, Bacon, Chaucer, Bunyan, Hallam, Seymour, Cranmer, Gaveston, Edgeworth, Jekyll, Smollett, Keats, Wolsey, Donne, Latimer, Gibbon.

Not only the names but the situations smack of English libraries. The unexpected return of Harriet Haslam to her too patently ungrieving family in *Men and Wives* suggests the return of Sir Thomas Bertram in *Mansfield Park*. The relationship between Felix and Sir Robert Bacon in *More Women Than Men* is like Lord Goring's with his father in *An Ideal Husband*. Mortimer Lamb's returning home because he had heard his brother's voice from miles away, calling his name, was certainly inspired by Jane Eyre's hearing Mr. Rochester's appeal from across the countryside. And do not Gaunt Lovat's dialogues with Sir Ransom Chace in *Darkness and Day* have a trace of Knightley's with Mr. Woodhouse in *Emma*? I doubt that Dame Ivy really intended these reminders. They are simply part and parcel, like the dimly outlined country houses and the nebulous servants' halls, of an English literary setting.

Dame Ivy does not need violent feelings to go with her violent events. She seems to feel that emotion in literature has been considerably overdone, that most humans are too self-absorbed to feel anything like the passions and jealousies so optimistically attributed to them by writers of fiction. Here is how Hereward's sons in *A God and His Gifts* react to his unconscious revelation:

> "What a story it is! It should not belong to real life."
> "It would be better in a book. I am sure I wish it was in one."

People, she appears to be saying, are pretty much the same the world over. They are milder than often thought, even when they commit murder. She puts one in mind of the newspaper quotes of a criminal's neighbors after some particularly brutal sex killing: "But he seemed just the kind of nice quiet boy you'd want your daughter to go out with!" Dame Ivy's characters are rarely capable of passion. When they are, like Harriet Haslam in *Men and Wives*, it may be fatal to them. They are sorry for themselves and act almost exclusively in what they deem their own best interests. They never die of broken hearts, and they are prone to greater dislikes than affections. What differentiates them from lower animals and gives them such dim glory as they may boast is the power of speech. It also gives them much of their trouble, for, as one character observes: "There would not be any subjects if we had not developed the power of speech. They are not really natural." Incest, for example, is unknown to beasts; it becomes a wrong only when a blood relationship is defined.

The true drama of the world, as Dame Ivy visualizes it, lies not in the conflict of passions, nor in love or hate or towering ambition, but in the effort of one individual to dominate others and in that of the others to resist him or her. The threatened majority tends to form an opposing mass, like a ring of musk oxen, offering a passive but effective block. The hateful Anna Donne in *Elders and Betters* is a rare example of evil triumphant. Usually the tyrant is quelled in the end, sometimes by death, sometimes by humiliation at exposed wrongdoing, sometimes even by a change of heart. In novel after novel this struggle is set forth: the despotic parent or grandparent against a cluster of clever murmuring younger family members who ultimately drive their would-be conqueror from the scene as crows in daylight drive off the marauding owl. The novels, taken together, may put one in mind of Bach concertos, repetitious in theme but never monotonous.

As so much of Dame Ivy's work comprises dialogue, and all that is greatest in it, I submit the following excerpts to win readers to the greater banquet of her oeuvre.

"Love does not count like admiration," said Gregory. "She loves Matthew. Children hate parents who love and do not admire them."

"But not parents children?" said Griselda.

"Children never admire their parents," said Gregory. "Parents have nothing deeper than love."

★   ★   ★

"At what age does one cease to be young?" said Gabriel.

"I shall always be young in heart," said Felix.

"That may be when we cease to be young," said Helen.

"When we are really young, I think our hearts age with the rest of us."

"Don't you like Christmas Day?"

"Well, Miss Nance, I could hardly be heard to say I didn't like it, being the day it is. But it tends to be more trouble than usual, with a feeling there ought to be less."

"True success seems to be effort and achievement without any reward. It is as bad as true kindness or honest advice or anything else of that kind."

"Being cruel to be kind is just ordinary cruelty with an excuse made for it," said Evelyn. "And it is right that it should be more resented, as it is."

"Why are people proud of expecting to die soon?" said Dudley to Mark. "I think it is humiliating to have so little life left."

"They are triumphant at having made sure of more life than other people. And they don't really think they will die."

"No, of course, they have got into the way of living. I see it is a lifelong habit."

"I know you think my heart is in the right place," said Eleanor, with a note of dryness.

"And why is that a poor compliment? It is the most fundamental of all things, in the sense that nothing counts without it."

"Perhaps that is why we never hear that a heart is anywhere else."

"The daily routine has to go on."

"That is known to seem so strange; it is supposed to seem that it should stop. But it might seem stranger if it did."

"We think our little failings have their own charm. And they have not. And they are great failings."

"Most people cannot relive the years. Only gifted people with empty lives can do so."

"I am a great admirer of simple goodness."

"I admire all goodness. I believe everyone does. And of course we like to say that kind hearts are more than coronets, as if we met both. But why is it better for being simple? I should admire complex goodness as much, though no one speaks about it."

"You have a great deal to be thankful for," said Fanshawe.

"That seems to mean people are unhappy. It is then that people say it to them."

"I have caused less shame to-day than was feared," said Selina. "I have failed, but it is a great failure."

"A great failure sounds nobler. And I suppose it must be. We never hear about mere or empty failure. Failure is never anything bad."

"I suppose criticism may be honest. Or is that the most unkindest cut of all?"

"Well, it is always a cut," said Ursula.

"Is it necessary to indulge in any kind of disparagement?"

"Well, it is a temptation," said Elton. "Look at your word, 'indulge.' And we are only told to make an exception of the dead."

"And it is no good to say behind people's backs what can never get round to them," said Ursula.

"Do we all regard ourselves as above the average?"

"Well, think what the average is."

"That hardly matters," said Flavia, "as everyone seems to be above it. Can you think of an average person?"

"Well, I would rather not think of one," said Ursula.

"Most people must be average," said Catherine, "or there would not be such a thing."

"Well, let us hope there is not," said her sister.

"So it is true that comedy and tragedy are mingled," said Adrian.

"Really it is all tragedy," said his sister. "Comedy is a wicked way of looking at it, when it is not our own."

"I have been surprised by the life-stories that have been unfolded to me."

"You might have been less so by the actual lives."

"Ah, to know all is to forgive all," said Rhoda.

"I confess I have not found it so, my lady. To forgive, it is best to know as little as possible."

"Wild horses would not drag the admission from me."

"Wild horses never have much success," said Lavinia. "Their history is a record of failure. And we do suggest a good deal for them."

"Ah, no one is the worse for our downfall. That must be our stay. Without it we were poor indeed."

"It sounds as if we should be poor with it. And some people must be the worse, if you mean we are in debt."

"We must not bring faint hearts to the stress of life. We must face our indebtedness, shoulder the burden and carry it with us. We will not bend beneath it, heavy in its way though it be. Is not that our own victory?"

"Yes, it is. We can be sure it would not be anyone else's."

"Ah, the humble part is the hard one. Gratitude is the rare thing to give. In a sense it is a gift. If we can give it, nothing is beyond us. To render it is the way to be unvanquished by it."

"It must be difficult to be vanquished," said Joanna. "I hardly see how anyone could be."

"You don't feel that marriage would mean a fuller life?"

"I don't want the things it would be full of."

"Great people always know how little they have achieved," said Joanna. "It does show how much they expected to."

William Gaddis

❧

I first came to know William Gaddis at a writers' conference in the Soviet Union in 1985. I had heard that he was shy and averse to publicity, but I found that this reputation was based only on his belief that a writer's life and personality should be as little as possible associated with his work. As a conferee he was both eloquent and precise.

Perhaps the most amusing contrast in our group was between him and Allen Ginsberg. Allen, shaggy and bearded, chanted his verse in loud emotional tones as he pounded a species of accordion that he always carried with him. Will, on the other hand, reserved and quiet, impeccably clad, with the patient composure of a man of the world and the piercing eye of a wit, spoke in measured tones of the small sales that a serious novelist might expect.

If Danielle Steel counted her sales in the millions while he had to make do with a few thousands, it was

First appeared in somewhat different form in *The New York Sunday Times Magazine*, November 15, 1987.

because, he explained, she wrote books and he wrote "literature." Asked for pointers as to future conferences, he glanced obliquely down the table at Allen and suggested that the novelists and poets be separated, so that the accordion should be heard only "down a long corridor, through a closed door."

Gaddis, who is considered by some critics to be the nearest thing to Herman Melville that our century has produced, who is almost a cult figure among students of English, is nonetheless not well-known to the wider reading public. His first two novels, *The Recognitions* and *JR*, published twenty years apart in 1955 and 1975, frightened off many readers by their length, erudition, and supposed difficulty. But this difficulty is much exaggerated by symbol and ambiguity hunters ("What can I do if people insist I'm cleverer than I think I am?" Gaddis asks with a shrug), and length and erudition become virtues when the stories are as interesting as his.

Gaddis has more to say to American readers today than any other novelist I can think of. Take just three fields in which his knowledge is significant: theology, painting, and corporate finance. Then consider the space devoted by the press in the 1980s to religious strife and revivalism, to art sales and art frauds, to stock-market chicanery and insider trading. Some critics have credited me as a novelist with a degree of familiarity in the last-named field, but I have treated it only in broad outlines and with a minimum of legal details. Gaddis could almost qualify as an expert witness in the trial of a malefactor.

★　　　★　　　★

For all his "relevance" (to use, with due apology, the sacred term of the 1960s) to our time, Gaddis is something of an antimodernist. His novels contain much merciless satire of the pretentious double-talk of literary cocktail parties and the inane pursuit of new art forms at any cost. Originality? Was that not what Eve was guilty of when she bit the apple?

Wyatt Gwyon, the painter protagonist of *The Recognitions*, quotes his old German teacher as saying:

> That romantic disease, originality, all around we see originality of incompetent idiots, they could draw nothing, paint nothing, just so the mess they make is original. . . . Even 200 years ago who wanted to be original, to be original was to admit that you could not do a thing the right way, so you could only do it your own way. When you paint you do not try to be original, only you think about your work.

And Stanley, the musician in the same novel, gives vent to a similar train of thought:

> How could Bach have accomplished all that he did? and Palestrina? the Gabrielis? . . . And how? with music written for the Church. Not written with obsessions of copyright foremost; not written to be played by men in worn dinner jackets, sung by girls in sequins, involved in wage disputes and radio rights, recording rights, union rights . . . not written to be punctuated by recommendations for headache remedies, stomach appeasers, detergents, hair oil . . . O God!

Yet Gaddis, for all the conservatism uttered by characters with whom he is in obvious sympathy, is one of the great innovative novelists of our age. "He comes very close to liberating his fiction (and one might even claim all fiction) from the nemesis of narrative, the Western mania for order and control," wrote Joel Dana Black in *In Recognition of William Gaddis*, a volume of appreciative essays published in 1984.

The new reader of a Gaddis novel may initially suppose that he is being introduced to a chaos in which the parts have little relation to one another or to the whole. But this is not the case. Each character and event is an integral part of a complex but interrelated whole. Does the whole compose an order that makes sense? The same question might be asked of our universe. The world that is subject to our senses, like a Gaddis novel, may be like a huge picture puzzle with no picture, in which a seemingly infinite number of pieces may be fitted together to form a glaze of white—or black.

Gaddis's parents were divorced when William, their only child, born in 1922, was three years old. From then on, the boy lived with his mother. She supported him by initially working as secretary to the president of the New York Steam Corporation; in time, she became an executive of the company. Because her work was demanding, Gaddis was sent from age five to thirteen to a boarding school in Berlin, Connecticut. After that, he returned to the family home in Massapequa, Long Island, where he attended high school until he entered Harvard College as a freshman in 1941.

Gaddis remained at Harvard for the four years of
World War II, being exempted from military service
because of a kidney disorder. He became president of
the *Lampoon*, the humorous and satirical undergraduate
magazine, contributing a large number of stories,
poems, essays, playlets, and theater and film reviews.
In his senior year, Gaddis and a drinking companion
were asked to resign from the college following a fracas
with the Cambridge police, an event perhaps anticipated by one of his *Lampoon* poems, in the style of
Tennyson's "Locksley Hall":

> I'll escape the alma mater,
> Rise above the madding throng;
> Join a band of vulgar gypsies
> And make my sordid song.

The next two years were spent in New York's
Greenwich Village while he worked as a fact checker on
The New Yorker magazine. His mother subsequently
rented out the house in Massapequa, giving him $100 a
month from the proceeds. With that, plus income from
temporary jobs, Gaddis was able to travel for the next
five years.

He first went to Mexico, in the spring of 1947, and
arrived in Panama City later that year, hoping for a job
on the newspaper *Panama-American*. When this failed to
materialize, he worked as a machinist's assistant on the
overhaul of the Miraflores locks of the Panama Canal. In
the evenings, clad in his white suit, he enjoyed the more
elegant society of the Union Club. But there was adven-
ture, too.

In 1948, Gaddis went up to Costa Rica during its two-week civil war, when José Figueres—a socialist landowner who was subsequently elected president—challenged the refusal of the ruling families to abide by the results of a popular election. Gaddis joined the insurgents and helped to keep open an airstrip for the delivery of supplies from Guatemala.

In the fall of that year, he went to Spain, where he remained for two years, traveling and studying art and church history, gathering material for and working on his first novel, *The Recognitions*. He arrived in Paris in 1950. It was a city that never dazzled him quite as it did so many of his fellow Americans ("Age cannot wither, nor custom stale her infinite vulgarity").

A year later, he made a short trip to North Africa before returning to New York to continue work on *The Recognitions*. An advance from Harcourt Brace & Company, plus fees from occasional writing assignments, enabled him to work through 1952 and 1953 to complete his big book. Its nearly 1,000 pages were published in 1955. Gaddis was thirty-two.

The reviews were not favorable, and the sales were small. There might have been some feeling in the literary establishment that Gaddis showed remarkable hubris in writing so long and difficult a work. In the *New York Times Book Review*, Granville Hicks complained that Gaddis "has so ostentatiously aimed at writing a masterpiece."

Most damning of all was Sterling North's review in the *New York World-Telegram*: "If I were so naïve as to believe in the devil I would say that young Mr. Gaddis had willingly sold his soul to achieve this Faustian first novel. What this sprawling, squalling, overwritten book needs above all is to have its mouth washed out with lye soap. It reeks of decay and filth and perversion and half-digested learning."

Poor Gaddis was almost crushed. Five years of work for that! In an interview with Zoltan Abadi-Nagy in the *Paris Review*, he says of that time of his life: "I almost think that if I'd got the Nobel Prize when *The Recognitions* was published, I wouldn't have been terribly surprised. I mean that's the grand intoxication of youth or what's a heaven for. And so the book's reception was a sobering experience, quite a humbling one, real life."

Wyatt Gwyon, the protagonist of *The Recognitions*, is the son of a Calvinist minister in New England who loses his mind in the intensity of his researches into pagan theologies. Wyatt escapes his ministerial calling and goes to Paris to paint. He marries Esther, a would-be writer, and returns to America, where he settles in Greenwich Village and becomes involved with a number of poets, playwrights, painters, and musicians, all drinking and drugging their way through a wasteland of compulsive modernism.

Wyatt turns for his inspiration to the great masters of the past, particularly the Flemish: Roger van der Weyden, Jan van Eyck, and Hugo van der Goes. Studying these painters with some of his father's intensity, he achieves a sense of identity with them that takes him ultimately down the road to forgery.

But Wyatt is no vulgar forger. In "recognizing" the genius of his predecessors, he brings himself into a relation with the past that gives a degree of form to the meaninglessness of the present. The novel is filled with these recognitions, flashes of intuition by which different characters become aware of archetypes in the past of their own personal experiences.

But if T. S. Eliot finds only "inexplicable glory" in the past, which he delights in contrasting with the tackiness of the present, Gaddis finds idiocy throughout the ages. Only in art, he seems to suggest, can man find redemption.

Wyatt's recognitions of his predecessors, then, go deeper than copying details. He studies van der Goes until he virtually becomes van der Goes. Like an ancient alchemist, he seeks to create gold out of baser metal, though he must have some gold to start with. He paints the pictures that the old masters ought to have painted. But when he falls into the hands of villains—Recktall Brown, the dealer, and Basil Valentine, the Jesuitical aesthete—and appends a false signature to a picture, he is hopelessly contaminated.

Wyatt goes mad at the end of the novel and sets about to destroy, under pretense of cleaning and restoring, the works of art in the monastery to which he has retreated. Does this cast doubt on the power of art to atone for the falsities of the world? Perhaps not altogether.

Right after the publication of *The Recognitions*, Gaddis married Pat Black, a young woman from North Carolina who had come to New York with the idea of a stage career. Their two children, Sarah and Matthew, were born in the next three years. But the poor reception of the novel, plus severe financial problems, exacerbated by the repeated vandalizations of the converted barn in Massapequa where he had done much of his writing, darkened what would have been a happy period of his life.

As literature would not provide a living for him and his family, Gaddis turned to commerce. From 1957 to 1961, he worked in public relations for Pfizer International, the pharmaceutical company, a job he despised.

His next job was more interesting. He worked for the U.S. Army, preparing documentary films for training and public relations. In 1964, however, with America's involvement in Vietnam intensified, Gaddis severed his army connection. He did freelance writing for industrial films and speechwriting for Eastman Kodak.

Reading one of these—a smooth, expertly prepared address on the utility and utilization of video aids in parochial schools—and contrasting it with the savage satire on the same subject in *JR*, his second novel, one marvels at the different functions to which Gaddis could adapt his skills.

The critical reception of *JR* in 1975 was gratifyingly different from the one that had greeted its predecessor. There was perhaps a note of contrition that the literary establishment had not recognized Gaddis's earlier book as a literary work of the first importance.

Even those critics who still found him on the lengthy side conceded his stature. He was described as a novelist "of Swiftian fury," "wildly satiric," "dazzling." The following spring, *JR* was given the National Book Award.

JR is indeed worthy of Swift. The sixth grade of a Long Island grammar school goes on a field trip to Wall Street, where the children are to be given the sensation of "investing in America" by being allowed to purchase one share of stock. JR, a scruffy eleven-year-old, demonstrates his financial acumen by cheating his classmates out of the share and using it to win a stockholder's suit.

With lease-backs and write-offs and tax deductions, he puts together a crazy but formidable corporate empire of junk merchandise and used-up properties that is a paradigm of the jumbled chaos of American financial life.

Irving Thalberg, the genius of Metro-Goldwyn-Mayer, was said to have sat alone in a darkened room while he trained his mind to become that of a thirteen-year-old girl—the mental age he deemed closest to that of the average American adult. Gaddis puts the level even lower.

In the *Paris Review*, he says of JR: "The reason he is eleven is because he is in this prepubescent age where he is amoral, with a clear conscience, dealing with people who are immoral, unscrupulous, which implies that they realize what scruples are but push them aside, whereas his good cheer and greed he considers perfectly normal. He thinks this is what you're supposed to do, and he is not going to wait around. . . ."

But how, even in a satire, could an eleven-year-old put together so gigantic a fortune? If it were all magic and fantasy, it would soon become a bore, particularly in a 726-page book. This is where Gaddis's knowledge of business affairs (unrivaled among American novelists except by Michael Thomas) stands him in such good

William Gaddis

stead. In turning the American dream inside out, he
wanted to have his facts right.

JR, he explains in the *Paris Review*, "buys defaulted
bond issues simply because they're cheap—it says
$1,000 up in the corner, but selling at seven cents on the
dollar, so he's getting them for $70 apiece. So it's simple,
cheerful greed. Then, when finally the corporation is
thrown into bankruptcy, and he emerges as the largest
bondholder, and they wipe out all of the stock, all the
equities, he becomes, then, the largest holder of preferred stock and takes control pretty much by default."

And so it goes, through a dozen or more fantastic but
basically credible deals. The capitalist system, which is
so often oblivious to sensitive morality, operates with
the enthusiasm of a child. Gaddis would preserve it. He
believes that free enterprise is the least dangerous eco-
nomic system yet devised by man, but he would regulate
it. He might make an excellent member of the Securities
and Exchange Commission.

That he knows the voice of the investment counselor is
shown in this dialogue between Edward Bast and his
financial adviser about the portfolio of the former's maid-
en aunts who simply want a little income to live on:

—See where we sold their telephone company right
here yes, and this Nobili you people have been buying
into, got them a block here at 31, averaged down with
another block here when it dropped to 23 and got them
out at 16, gives them a nice little tax loss.
—Oh.
—Yes and here, another nice tax loss in Ampex
haven't we, averaged down at 20 yes and again at 14, the

rate management was handing out false figures to the analysts there was enough to make your hair curl, able to get them out at 6 though before it hit bottom.

—Oh what was, bottom . . .

—Selling at around 5 yes and it may be one of the better bargains right now if you think your aunts would . . .

—No but, but what's this one, FAS . . .

—Famous Artists yes, correspondence courses in the arts photography that sort of thing, thought they might find it a bit more congenial than these humdrum industrials.

—Oh, is it a tax loss too?

—No matter of fact they may enjoy a complete write-off with this one.

Surrounding JR is a huge cast of adult characters, who are lured to his corporate empire by the hope that there may be something in it for them. It is not always just money that they seek. It is understanding, appreciation, acceptance. But the society in which they live has few rewards to offer them but money, and not very much of that—just enough, often, to corrupt them.

JR himself, wistful, likable, essentially well-meaning, is the only one not contaminated by the avarice of the corporate operations, but that is because he is totally insensitive. When one of his teachers, Amy Joubert, who comes as close as any of the adult characters to being a person of goodwill, tries to make him see something other than profit in the world around him she fails.

—Just stop for a minute! she caught an arm round his shoulders—just stop and look . . . !

William Gaddis

—What? at what . . .

—At the evening, the sky, the wind, don't you ever just stop sometimes and look? . . . Is there a millionaire for that?

As is said in David Madden's anthology *Rediscoveries*, the most frightening implication of this massive comedy is that JR is the sanest character of the novel. Perhaps that is because he is the simplest—one might actually hope to make something better of him. It is admittedly a frail hope to put in the rushing path of the entropy of our civilization.

Gaddis's techniques to express his terrifying conception of this entropy—the tendency of a system to disorder—is to create his novel almost entirely by conversations in which the speakers are not immediately identified. The reader must make do without the usual exposition of facial expressions or mental reactions. He has no way of verifying whether a character is speaking falsely or sincerely or sarcastically, except by what the character actually says.

However, this makes it sound much more difficult than it is. One soon picks up the style, certainly the clichés, of the individual speaker, and after a bit one reads the dialogue almost as easily as if it were accompanied by the "he said" or "she said" of conventional fiction.

What then, it will be asked, does Gaddis gain by putting his reader through this exercise? He gains the eerie effect of identifying our civilization with all of its jargons.

Reading *JR*, I feel at times as if I were lying alone on a desolate plain under a dark cloudy sky from which come the mumbles and throbs of human speech in every sort of dialect and slang, replete with self-pity, smugness, officiousness, swagger—in short, every banality the brain of man can devise to evade thought.

In *Carpenter's Gothic* (1985), the third of Gaddis's novels, he has limited himself to a mere 262 pages and has set himself the task of observing the dramatic unities of time and place. The action occurs within the span of a few days in a Victorian house on the Hudson, rented by Paul and Elizabeth Booth. She is an heiress, but her fortune is tied up in endless litigation, much to the disgust of her glib, hucksterish husband, a public relations agent who is helping his only client, Reverend Ude, a television preacher, to develop an evangelical movement in Africa.

The plot embraces much of the madness of the modern world: exploited African mines and natives, corrupt politicians, popular religion, unscrupulous intelligence agents, a murderous search for concealed geological surveys and, finally, Armageddon. It is the grimmest of Gaddis's novels, being concerned, though always comically, with the tragedy of human stupidity.

Gaddis shatters the silence and isolation of the old house on the river with the sounds of telephone, radio, and television, so that it seems at times more like a bunker at the front than a secluded villa. The violent death that comes in the end to the heroine is a horrific comment on the illusion of immunity that she had desperately sought.

★   ★   ★

William Gaddis

Gaddis's first marriage ended in divorce, in 1967, as did his second, to Judith Thompson, a decade later. He blames these failures on the terrible pressures of trying to earn a living while writing two monumental novels, and on the frustration of his small sales, which continued even after all the awards and plaudits. It made him, he frankly admits, a difficult person to live with. If this was so, there is little sign of it today. Living in New York and Long Island, Gaddis and his charming and brilliant companion, Muriel Oxenberg Murphy, seem to enjoy immensely each other and a life of work and wide traveling. He has just published (1994) his fourth novel, *A Frolic of His Own*, a devastating and hilarious satire on America's obsession with lawsuits, and has been named "New York State Writer" by Governor Cuomo for the years 1994–1995.

The Tragic Mood
in Early Jacobean Drama

❧

Some years ago I had the pleasure of rehearsing for public television a play that I had written about a New York corporation law firm. The actors, mostly young and employed in "soaps," had never had the smallest experience with lawyers. They were virgin alike to the tender offer, the capital loss carryover, and the generation-skipping trust. Their dress and speech seemed as far from Wall Street as Tasmania or the Antarctic. And yet, within a scant few hours of reading their parts, I was suddenly transported to my own office in downtown Manhattan. For these young people had immediately seized the hang of it. Like mimes who follow an unconscious Pantaloon down the street, aping the shake of his head or the shuffling of his feet, they knew at once and promptly reproduced their man.

There are still the benighted who insist that Shakespeare couldn't have known what King Lear or Richard II was like unless he had been a prince or a great noble, someone, in short, with daily access to royalty.

Never will you hear them argue that he must have been a drunken tinker because he created Christopher Sly or a fathead steward because he conceived Malvolio. No, according to these, the only life that *must* be learned at first hand, if it is to be reproduced in drama, is that of a monarch or aristocrat. And yet isn't it obvious that just the opposite is true? The lives of the great and powerful are open to everybody. Even in our day every school child reads about the private doings of the president of the United States or the queen of England. It was probably easier for Shakespeare to imagine life at Hampton Court than anywhere else in England.

Actually, if you knew nothing whatever of the identity of the author of the thirty-seven plays in the Shakespearian canon, and had to supply his portrait by deduction and supposition, or by making up a kind of composite man from the biographies of all the contemporary English dramatists, you would probably come up with an actor-manager, or at least a man who had spent much of his life hanging about theatres. Who else, after all, would recognize so clearly the different walks of society, be abreast of every literary fashion, know the talk of the town and how to satirize it, and, most importantly, smell in the local air the prevailing currents of whatever is considered at the moment funniest, or saddest, or most romantic, or most tragic?

The so-called Non-Stratfordians are apt to concentrate exclusively on the plays of the man we call Shakespeare, without concerning themselves with his fellow dramatists. Yet Shakespeare cannot be properly separated from these. If you read each of his plays with what was staged at the same time by other playwrights, you will be struck at how closely he followed the fashion of the day and how much he resembled his contemporaries in plot, treatment, and even verse. It is only in the *degree* of his genius that he transcends the rest. There is no explaining genius—it just happens, in all types and classes of humans—but you don't get any closer to an answer by supposing him an earl. Indeed, you have simply added to your hurdles the inhibiting quality of rank on free expression.

The late Elizabethan and early Jacobean dramatists addressed themselves spiritedly to the same themes: madness, murder, cuckoldry, ambition, treason, and passion, set in palaces and graveyards, often in Italy. Yet not one of these poets was either a peer or a pauper.

Francis Beaumont was the son of a knight and judge. He studied law at the Inner Temple. His collaborator, John Fletcher, was the son of the bishop of Bristol. Christopher Marlowe was a cobbler's son who received a scholarship at Cambridge on condition that he study divinity. Philip Massinger was the son of a gentleman in the service of the earl of Pembroke. Ben Jonson and Thomas Middleton were the sons of bricklayers. John Marston was the son of a lawyer and became one himself. Cyril Tourneur was a diplomatic courier and perhaps a soldier, as was Chapman. John Webster may have been an actor.

If the list covers a wide range of English society it is immediately notable that it excludes the top and the bottom rungs of the ladder. It has plenty of variety, but that variety fades before the greatest common denominator of a professional connection with the London theatre, either as playwright, actor, or manager. It is this that gives to these writers a homogeneity to which Shakespeare was no exception.

Certainly even those of the dramatists who admired and worked with Shakespeare did not consider him a star apart from themselves. John Webster, for example, did not even rank him among the first of his fellow playwrights. He wrote:

> For my own part I have ever truly cherished my good opinion of other men's worthy labors, especially of that full and heightened style of Master Chapman; the labored and understanding works of Master Jonson; the no less worthy composures of the both worthily excellent Master Beaumont and Master Fletcher; and lastly (without wrong last to be named) the right happy and copious industry of Master Shakespeare, Master Decker and Master Heywood.

Shakespeare, like the others, gave his audiences pretty much what they wanted. When he was under the influence of Marlowe (whom he called his shepherd), he wrote *Titus Andronicus* and *Richard III*, and toward the end of his dramatic career he emulated, in *Cymbeline* and *The Winter's Tale*, the romantic tragedies of Beaumont and Fletcher. Some of his biographers have attempted to attribute his changes of subject matter and treatment not to current fashion but to alterations in his mood. They see *Measure for Measure* and *Troilus and Cressida* as the products of a period of mental depression when the treachery of man and the infidelity of woman had become actually nauseating to him. But I find this a naïve conception of the workings of the creative mind. I suspect that Shakespeare was at his happiest when he wrote his best scenes, and that, after killing off Cordelia and Lear, he may have got drunk with Cyril Tourneur and roared with laughter over a discussion of the goriest parts of *The Revenger's Tragedy*. An audience may take a work of art for real, but not an artist.

The first six years of the reign of James I (1603–1609) were a golden era in theatre history, producing not only three of Shakespeare's finest tragedies, but several of the greatest of his contemporaries, all marked with a curious similarity of mood. From Shakespeare we have *Othello*, *King Lear*, *Macbeth*, and *Cymbeline*; from Tourneur, *The Revenger's Tragedy*; from Middleton, *Women Beware Women*; from Beaumont and Fletcher, *The Maid's Tragedy*; and from Webster, *The White Devil* and perhaps *The Duchess of Malfi*. We find in these dramas a preoccupation with evil, often senseless, even motiveless evil, sometimes actually demented.

Consider the appalling number of crimes portrayed in early Jacobean tragedy and seek the reason for them. Is there any? Vendice in *The Revenger's Tragedy* does not have to kill nearly as many people as he does to avenge the murder of his beloved; his need for blood becomes a compulsion driving him on to massacre. Similarly, in *Women Beware Women* the entire ducal court is ultimately sucked into a senseless whirlpool of killing. Brachiano in *The White Devil* seems more interested in murdering his wife and his mistress's husband than he is in being freed to marry Vittoria. There is something crazy in his cruelty to his wretched spouse, who insists on taking on her own shoulders the blame for his infidelities. Why in *The Winter's Tale* does Leontes destroy his family in a fit of jealousy over courtesies between his wife and his best friend that wouldn't have raised even Othello's eyebrow? And why do the duchess of Malfi's brothers so fiendishly resent her harmless, private marriage?

And take Macbeth. He plots the murder of Duncan, as A. C. Bradley has pointed out, as if it were a kind of grim duty. Never once does he anticipate the smallest pleasure from the crown that he will wrest from its lawful owner. And as for Iago in *Othello* . . . well, we know about Iago. He has no motive for his villainy, or rather he gives too many. He is the only one of the lot who seems to be perplexed by what Coleridge called his "motiveless malignity."

Why then did Iago and the other villains have no motives or insufficient ones for their crimes? Of course it is important to recognize that sometimes seemingly perverse or arbitrary conduct derives from the playwright's fidelity to the source of his plot. His audience, equally familiar with it, would tolerate as the excesses of romantic lore actions that shock later generations. Thus the old tale of the loving husband who is willing to subject his unwarned spouse to an attempted seduction by a villain to win a wager on her chastity justified Posthumous in *Cymbeline*, and the popularity of the "bed plot" exonerated Helena in *All's Well That Ends Well* from the charge of indelicacy in taking another woman's place in a dark adulterous rendezvous with her husband. But gratuitous villainy was just as horrible to Jacobean audiences as to modern ones. Why was it that playwrights of the era made such frequent use of it?

I have read arguments that the tragic mood of the first half dozen years of the reign of James I may be attributed to the corruption of that monarch's court and the contrast it offered to the halcyon era of the great Elizabeth. Certainly today we Americans are very conscious of the lifestyles of our presidents. But before these may be said to affect the mood of artists, they must strike at something fundamental in the moral structure of our society. The charm of a Kennedy, the bluntness of a Johnson, the blandness of a Reagan will not have much effect on writers. On the other hand the assassination of Kennedy, the warmongering of Johnson, and the crimes of Nixon may. Neither the old Elizabeth nor the young James indulged in wars or crimes; neither was murdered, and I can hardly believe that the difference between their courts struck very deeply into the imagination of the bards at the Mermaid Tavern. Besides, they could have viewed those differences differently. Some might have seen a glorious and inspiring virgin queen succeeded by an ignoble megalomaniac who slobbered over his minions. Others might have seen a vigorous and down-to-earth young Scot uniting two great nations on the demise of a bewigged and toothless old hag.

The moods of dramatic works need not reflect personal, political, or even social events; they may be simply the product of intellectual fashions, and the wind of fashion in this era blew from Italy, or from the legend of Italy.

Most of the tragedies here cited are set in more or less contemporary Italian towns. Probably none of the playwrights had ever set foot on the peninsula, so there was nothing to correct or modify the glittering images of Florence or Rome or Venice in their minds. Renaissance Italy was a romance of marble palaces and elegant, remorseless villains, of beautiful women in rich, jeweled brocade gowns, of the clash of steel on steel, of passion, hate, and murder. Vernon Lee in *Euphorion* points out that, oddly enough, whereas Italy in Jacobean literature is shown as a land of violence and sudden death, in *Italian* literature of the same period it appears as calm, serene, almost benign. But Londoners in the reign of James I were not interested in exact delineation, particularly where foreign parts were concerned. They wanted a good show. They wanted the double pleasure of reveling in blood for two hours and then feeling superior, as they left the theatre, to the alien monsters they had just been watching. Those things couldn't happen, after all, in Merrie England. They could only happen in the land of wops and dagos, or whatever the contemporary pejorative term was for Mediterranean folk.

The Duchess of Malfi is the perfect expression of this tragic mood. The duchess, one of the loveliest of Jacobean heroines, moves across the scene with a radiant patience and gaiety. She is perfectly blameless of all the horrors that befall her, perfectly guiltless. She has secretly married a good and worthy man who is below her in rank. For this she and her children are horribly tortured and slaughtered. That is all, really, that happens. The tragedy is contained simply in the beauty of the victim; beauty of soul as well as body, a beauty that transcends the evil of the world around her and finally overwhelms and damns her destroyers.

Similarly, in *King Lear* the king is faultless. Oh, yes, he is an old fool to give up his kingdom to two such horrible daughters, and on the basis of such a silly test, but as I read the play he is meant to be showing the first signs of senility. He is one of the few Shakespearian characters whose age is given us, and eighty was a very great age for the time. Besides, there is no suggestion in the speeches of the repentant Lear, or in those of any of the other characters, that the old man was showing anything but the poor judgment of his time of life. It is the same with the duchess of Malfi in wedding her steward. Yet Lear, like the duchess, is subjected to the most hideous trials, and he triumphs over his enemies in the end, not by physical force but by moral beauty. When, as a captive of the forces of evil, he puts a protective arm about Cordelia's shoulders and says, "Come, let's away to prison; we two will sing like birds in a cage," we feel that he is at last the victor and has escaped his foe.

So there it is, the mood of the day: to see the world as a futile battlefield where ignorant armies clash by night. *Troilus and Cressida* is an exact example of this: the final curtain falls on a darkening battlefield where Troilus, half-crazed by disillusionment in love and by grief over the death of Hector, continues to seek his own extinction in combat.

Let me in conclusion return once more to the English poets' obsession with Italy and its supposed villains so vividly described by Vernon Lee.

There is for these men no fatality save the evil nature of man, no justice save the doubling of crime, no compensation save revenge; there is for Webster and Ford and Tourneur and Marston no heaven above, wrathful but placable; there are no gods revengeful but just; there is nothing but this blood-stained and corpse-strewn earth, defiled by lust-burnt and death-hungering men, felling each other down and trampling on one another blindly in the eternal darkness which surrounds them. The world of these great poets is not the open world with its light and its air, its purifying storms and lightnings: it is the darkened Italian palace, with its wrought-iron bars preventing escape; its embroidered carpets muffling the foot steps; its hidden, suddenly yawning trap-doors; its arras hangings concealing masked ruffians; its garlands of poisoned flowers; its long suites of untenanted darkened rooms, through which the wretch is pursued by the half-crazed murderer; while below, in the cloistered court, the clanking armor and stamping horses, and above, in the carved and gilded hall, the viols and lutes and cornets make a cheery triumphant concert, and drown the cries of the victim.

But there is also the duchess, the dying duchess of Malfi, who has "youth and a little beauty." Perhaps it was almost enough.

The Inner FDR

❧

Along the walls of the main hall of the classroom building of Groton School were hung, in chronological order, the framed autographed letters of the presidents of the United States. Since Theodore Roosevelt, whose sons had attended the school, these letters had all been addressed to the headmaster. As a fourth-former in the winter of 1933, I eagerly awaited the hanging of the letter of Franklin Delano Roosevelt, Groton '00. Would he write that he had been inspired by this same collection in his student days to become in afterlife the great statesman that he had become? What a climax!

But when the letter arrived, it seemed, at least to a fifteen-year-old, rather an anticlimax. The newly inaugurated president recorded that the collection had indeed inspired him to become what he had later become—a collector. I did not realize how neatly he was spoofing the general expectation.

First appeared in somewhat different form in *The New York Review of Books*, November 21, 1985.

Later in my academic career I discovered that the FDR twist could work the other way just as neatly. He came to the University of Virginia in the spring of 1940 to deliver the address at the law school graduation of his son Franklin. Professor Leslie Buckler of the law faculty boarded the official train to greet the Roosevelts and sit with them while the ramp for the president's wheelchair was put in place. It was natural that the topic of law degrees should be introduced, and the president, while expressing his satisfaction at Franklin's graduation, nonetheless pointed out that in his day a degree had not been a requisite to taking the New York Bar Examinations and that he had become a practicing attorney without finishing at Columbia Law. After a pause, Leslie Buckler replied that his own situation had been similar: returning from the war in Europe, he had been allowed to take the Maryland Bar without going back to school. There was a moment's silence, and then the famous laugh rang out. "But you're not president of the United States!"

If one were to take a national poll asking which were the three greatest presidents, I think it likely that Washington, Lincoln, and Franklin Roosevelt would be the ones chosen. Jefferson, according to many historians, left us too shockingly unprepared for the War of 1812; Jackson's reforms seem mild enough in the light of social changes to come; and a greater modern awareness of Theodore Roosevelt's jingoism has tended to trivialize his once heroic image. But Washington's unchallenged position as our founding father has saved him from later carping; Lincoln has been deified and FDR continues to dominate the chronicle of our century.

When the young FDR, then Assistant Secretary of the

Navy, called on Henry Adams, it is ironic that the venerable sage of Lafayette Square should have said to him: "Young man, I have lived in this house many years and seen the occupants of that white house across the square come and go, and nothing that you minor officials or the occupants of that house can do will affect the history of the world for long." Adams was talking to a future occupant of that house who would disprove the claim.

Obviously, there were factors that helped to establish the enduring fame of FDR other than his peculiar genius. The greatest depression and the greatest war of the century occurred in his administrations, and that we pulled out of the first and were victorious in the second was not entirely his doing. Also he had the luck of having a First Lady more loved and more active than any other to that date. And, of course, he was elected president four times, twice as many as any other. But it was still his broad smile, his jaunty air of optimism, his confident and silver-toned speeches that gave the world hope, and justified hope, in its darkest hours.

Both the stories with which I started this piece suggest FDR's persistent consciousness of the excitement and drama of his great position, and a study of the three excellent additions to the swelling body of literature about him—*Before the Trumpet*, by Geoffrey C. Ward; *FDR: The New York Years*, by Kenneth S. Davis; and *FDR*, by Ted Morgan—has led me to speculate that a peculiar and very private sense of personal drama and destiny may be the key to the elusive character of the thirty-second president.

Ward quotes Eleanor as writing, somewhat resentfully, after her husband's death: "I was one of those who served his purposes." FDR had no real confidants, she maintained, certainly not herself. No human being ever fully shared his inner life.

This was true, even from his boyhood. Morgan writes:

> He had to fight to get his locks trimmed and to graduate from dresses and kilts. He learned that there was a part of himself he could not reveal to his mother, and acquired an opaque core, a sort of inner armor. It was a matter of survival. . . .
>
> It was at his mother's knee that he learned the protective ambiguity that so many of his associates would later comment upon. As the brain truster Rexford Tugwell put it, "He was the kind of man to whom those who wanted him convinced of something—usually something in their own interest—could talk and argue and insist, and come away believing that they had succeeded, when all that happened was that he had been pleasantly present."

After his affair with Lucy Mercer, FDR's relationship with Eleanor became more of a political partnership than a marriage. His children he always loved, but they were usually away and apt to give him more headaches than help with their divorces and speeding tickets and business problems. Louis Howe—in Davis's phrase that "untidy, irritable, asthmatic, chain-smoking little man"—and his secretary "Missy" LeHand were obsessively devoted to their boss, but idolatry does not make for true intimacy. The president accepted the offer of their lives gratefully, knowing that his success was all the return they expected. The Brain Trust, Moley,

Tugwell, Berle, et al., representing, as Davis puts it, "a historic attempt to bridge the gap between Intelligence and Power," stimulated and excited him, but they were essentially co-workers. As for his friends, they were for relaxation: Vincent Astor for fishing, his old college friend Livingston Davis for jokes and (in earlier days) for girls. FDR liked people in quantity, at parties, for banter, for story swapping, for general hilarity. Harry Hopkins came nearest to establishing a closer tie, but even that was mostly professional.

Yet I suspect he was not lonely: he did not need intimacy. He may even have shunned it. A satisfaction greater than that offered by people may have been supplied by a romantic vision of himself in history, a sense of his destiny that never left him, even in the terrible days of polio, a vision in which America was seen lapped by the blue waves of seas on which rode beautiful naval vessels and covered with rich valleys and streams and productive farms—he was always more of a Jeffersonian than a Hamiltonian, inclined to find the "good life" in the agricultural countryside as opposed to the wicked city. It was a vision, I suspect, whose setting was reproduced in prints and paintings and stamps, most of all stamps, so clear, so precise, so detailed yet so idealized, affirming America as a peaceful and democratic polity, an America that was waiting for a successor to Cousin Theodore.

This sustained inner identification of himself with the nation could have been a kind of artistic creation. He conformed himself to it, in appearance, in language, in manner, surrounding himself with beautiful and appropriate props: naval paintings and prints, fully rigged ship models, English political cartoons, a million stamps. The knowledge of history that he accumulated was prodigious. Adolf Berle said that he could tell you about naval construction, constitutional law, the story of coins, the ability of white men to live in the tropics—he could tell you about any concrete subject, it seemed, but had little interest in abstract ideas, their analysis, their contradictions. It was only natural that he should turn to people like Howe and LeHand who may have glimpsed the vision behind the style. Did any of his family really sense it? How could the verve of his conversations or the brilliance of his speeches have been appreciated by the author of "My Day"? For even the banalities of that column failed to exhaust the armory of clichés that Eleanor had amassed to combat the social evils of her time.

At first things came too easily for FDR. It must have seemed that the vision of himself in history could almost be left to realize itself. As Morgan puts it: "Before polio he walked along flower-strewn paths. Men came to him offering valuable prizes: Would he like to be state senator, or assistant secretary of the Navy? Would he like to run for vice president? There was an embarrassment of riches." And as Eleanor once said: "If something was unpleasant and he didn't want to know about it he just ignored it. I think he always thought that if you ignored a thing long enough, it would settle itself."

It was not only the polio that brought him to deeper revaluations of his character and destiny; it was the affair with Lucy Mercer when for the only time in his life he found himself tempted to throw up his political career and family for the gratification of a passion. He resisted it, gaining some of the strength that he was to need a few years later in the struggle with infantile paralysis. And when he emerged from the temptations of despair it was to find his old vision enhanced, even more powerful, as we can infer from Morgan's description of him at the Democratic Convention of 1924 when he nominated Al Smith in the "Happy Warrior" speech:

> Then came the moment when he had to walk alone. Releasing Jimmy's arm, he took the second crutch and moved across the stage, the crowd almost holding its breath as it watched. Putting aside his crutches, he grabbed the lectern, threw back his head and smiled into the spotlight's glare.
>
> Here was a man of American ancestry older than the nation itself, a man with a background of Cambridge Square, bearing a famous name, who had dragged his crippled body into the steaming convention hall to make a bid for a second-generation American born and bred in the East Side slums—surely this was what the framers of the Constitution had had in mind.

It was, anyway, what FDR had had in mind. A man who lives alone with a vision will be tempted to be his own moral judge. FDR believed in God, but religion to him was a very private matter; he avoided public worship because he did not like people to stare at him while he prayed. He may have regarded God as a kind of senior partner who did not really want to be consulted in pragmatic political decisions where the end (the vision) justified a very broad category of means.

Certainly FDR went very far with the latter. It is sad to learn that he denied Judge Joseph Proskauer any credit (except for the quotation from Wordsworth) in the writing of the "Happy Warrior" speech, his own greatest triumph up to that time. It now appears that Proskauer not only wrote every word of the address, but that FDR objected strongly to the text and agreed very reluctantly to use it at the last minute. He lied in a speech where he claimed to have written the constitution of Haiti. When he was Assistant Secretary of the Navy he lied in a congressional investigation of the navy's use of its men to entrap homosexuals, denying that he knew that the entrappers were instructed, if necessary, to engage in sexual acts with suspects. And as president he did not hesitate to use the tax power to smite his enemies while shielding his friends from its impact. Thus he spared Lyndon Johnson from prosecution by the Internal Revenue Service in the very smelly audit of the Brown & Root construction firm, which had surreptitiously financed Johnson's campaign for the Senate in 1941. But he pressed for an all-out investigation of Moe Annenberg for tax fraud, which resulted in the old man's conviction and jail sentence. When Annenberg rose from publishing the *Daily Racing Form* to become the owner of the *Philadelphia Inquirer*, he attacked the New Deal. Roosevelt told J. Edgar Hoover that Annenberg's group was out to "get" Harold Ickes if he came to Philadelphia. "I want Moe Annenberg for dinner," he told Henry Morgenthau, Jr., and he got him.

Of course, this protean side of FDR's nature could be a great political asset. As Morgan says, he adopted a position of deliberate changeability that allowed him to hold contradictory views simultaneously, juggling apples and oranges until the time was ripe for decision. Norman

Thomas, who regarded him as the greatest threat to socialism of the century, charged that he failed to make essential, internal connections between facts. Davis's reply to this is that as an essential man of action FDR had less faith in the need to correlate items of information than he had in the signs and portents presented to him through his senses. "He collected facts, including other people's expressed ideas, as he did stamps and naval prints." There they were, stored away in his remarkable memory, to be used when circumstances called, rather than woven into a systematized body of knowledge.

FDR's ultimate protection against the extremes to which his pragmatism might otherwise have led him lay in his sense of the nature and fragility of his own power. He knew, as Morgan expresses it, that he could maintain this power only so long as he made himself "the embodiment both of the collective will and the moral compact." Perhaps that is what I have called his "vision." Davis offers a touching picture of this usually self-sufficient and practical romantic turning at last to his "spiritual partner." When his son James was helping him to bed shortly after his election in 1932 he uttered one of his rare expressions of innermost feeling, "an almost unique revelation that what he felt was a fear of personal inadequacy in the face of personal challenge":

> "I'm just afraid I may not have the strength to do this job," he said. "After you leave me tonight, Jimmy, I am going to pray. I am going to pray that God will help me, that He will give me the strength and the guidance to do this job and to do it right. I hope you will pray for me, too, Jimmy."

The Waste Land
Without Pound

❧

At a lunch for the advisory committee of the *Dictionary of Literary Biography*, I told Lola Szladits, curator of the Berg Collection at the New York Public Library, that I had a heresy to confess. I impenitently clung to the opinion that Ezra Pound might have done a disservice to T. S. Eliot when he excised certain passages from *The Waste Land*. Since Ms. Szladits had an important part in publishing these deleted sections in Valerie Eliot's 1971 edition of her husband's manuscripts, I had assumed that she shared the prevailing academic view that Pound's maieutic hand had been a happy one. To my surprise I discovered that she agreed with me.

In my younger days I read everything suggested that might shed light on *The Waste Land*. I studied Jessie Weston's *From Ritual to Romance*; I pored through Frazer; I learned the constitution of the tarot pack; I

First appeared in *The New York Review of Books*, October 11, 1984.

searched libraries until I found a tattered copy of Countess Marie Larisch's *My Past*, and in London I even stood under the bell tower at St. Mary Woolnoth's to check the "dead sound on the final stroke of nine." There wasn't one. But diverting as these investigations proved, they did not shed much more light on the poem than Eliot's own footnotes about ancient fertility rites and their significance in the legend of the Holy Grail.

What was I left with, then, but a dazzling succession of images? Should these be enough? If there were a basic meaning to the poem, other than what Eliot himself had given it ("a personal and wholly insignificant grouse against life"), might it not be in the line "These fragments I have shored against my ruins"?

But when I read the manuscripts it seemed to me that Eliot was doing more than shoring together fragments. He appeared to be sampling lives of little people who picked their way about the ruins of older civilizations, unable, because of illiteracy, ignorance, or simple preciousness, to make profitable use of these shards.

I am not suggesting that one should do a Viollet-le-Duc restoration of the poem as Eliot might have conceived it had he never met Pound. He approved of all of Pound's emendations, and never afterward, so far as I know, suggested any dissatisfaction with them. *The Waste Land*, as published in 1922, must stand as a finished work, and even I will admit that Pound helped to give it conciseness and unity of mood. But it is still an entrancing game to browse through the manuscripts and speculate on what Eliot may have initially had in mind.

As I see it, *The Waste Land* originally comprised three basic elements: (1) the quotations, or semiquotations, that invoke the great literature and art of the past; (2) descriptions of the aridity and cultural poverty of the post–World War I era; and (3) dramatic episodes about individuals: average, flawed souls lost in a world they cannot understand.

Of the dramatic episodes, five in number initially, Pound deleted three. "The Burial of the Dead" was intended to open with a group of drunks loose on the town—London with overtones of Boston—who go to a music hall, flounder into a brothel, collide with the police, boast of their political connections, and end up having a running race on the sidewalk. Behind their noisy, fretful efforts to create an atmosphere of cheer and bravado lies the disapproving gloom of a city that has no use for them. Their feeble bleats will soon be extinguished in the engulfing night of nothingness.

The second eliminated episode concerns a day in the life of Fresca, a fashionable London bluestocking. It is conceived in the style of *The Rape of the Lock*, and its removal deprives us of an era in the literary scope that the poem embraces. Fresca, who has been nurtured on the lacquered prose of Symonds, Pater, and Vernon Lee, and who reads Samuel Richardson on the john, is the last word in literary affectation. She is also something of a tramp who dreams of "pleasant rapes." But she counter-balances the typist at the end of "The Fire Sermon" who is drearily seduced by the "young man carbuncular."

The third cut episode, whose excision is the one that most disturbs me, is that of the long fishing voyage and shipwreck in the North Atlantic that was taken from "Death by Water," leaving only the brief but beautiful passage about Phlebas the Phoenician. There is a pathetic passage in the notes to the manuscript edition where Eliot asks Pound if Phlebas must "go," too. But Pound spared him.

The action in the voyage is seen through the eyes of one of the fishermen not otherwise described, for here we are not concerned, as in the other episodes, with personalities (average weaklings in a crumbling society) but with human beings in a group, a bewildered, terrified herd. It is the joint experience of being lost in a strange sea with nothing but horror ahead that Eliot imbues with some of the mystery and awe of *The Rime of the Ancient Mariner*.

The manuscript ends with a series of poems, stanzas, fragments, and individual lines that were evidently rejected by Pound before Eliot had even decided where to place them in the whole. One of these, "The Death of a Saint Narcissus," a perfect little entity in itself, concerns a holy man's obliteration of his virulent ego that makes him identify himself with his beautiful victims, actual or imagined: the shining fish he has caught or the girl he has mentally raped. Eliot may have intended to include it in "What the Thunder Said," but it could go into any of the sections. This is also true of "Exequy," which brings a note of Keats and Shelley to the work; "Elegy," which invokes the "always inconvenient" dead; and the horrifying "Dirge," where the drowned Bleistein is consumed by lobsters ("scratch, scratch, scratch"). The presence of these virtually independent poems, one of which was submitted as such to a periodical, may be evidence that Eliot originally conceived *The Waste Land* as an even looser medley than it ultimately became.

There is, however, little question where he intended to place the longest of these additional pieces: "The Death of the Duchess." It would have come after the opening description of the lady's bedchamber in "A Game of Chess." One of the lady's identities is with Webster's duchess of Malfi, who loved and married her faithful steward and was murdered by her jealous and perhaps incestuous brother. This powerful, romantic story, set in the hard golden glare of the Italian Renaissance, is contrasted with an unconsummated affair between a nervous, fretful society woman of our time and a timorous epicene character who might be a clone of Prufrock. The reader would have been introduced to the splendor of the duchess's chamber, then switched to the dullness and banality of modern Hampstead with its birdlike people with dog eyes drinking tea, and then to the steward watching his querulous friend brushing her fiery hair, until finally the glory of Jacobean passion is eaten away by modern do's and don't's, why's and why-not's, and the episode can end in a closed car and a game of chess.

It seems to me that an expanded *Waste Land* would be more coherent. I suppose my basic difference with Pound boils down to the fact that, liking the poem so much, I simply want more of it. And now it may be time, in all humility, to recall that Eliot, who was almost as fine a critic as he was a poet, dedicated the work to the friend and collaborator whom he described as *"il miglior fabbro."*

Babylon Revisited

Gore Vidal's American Trilogy

In the beginning of Gore Vidal's novel *Hollywood*, the "Duchess," as the consort of Ohio senator Warren G. Harding is affectionately known, visits the Washington salon of the astrologist Madame Marcia to read her husband's horoscope. The visit has been arranged by Harding's henchman, Harry Daugherty, who is pushing him for the Republican nomination in 1920. Daugherty believes that his candidate will be nominated and elected, and he expects that Madame Marcia, who is consulted by the greatest in the land, will predict this, and that her prediction will be a good way of preparing the Duchess for her future role. Only Harding's hour and date of birth have been supplied to the functioning sorceress, but since she has instant access to the *Congressional Directory*, a glance could allow her to match the date to the man. Or has Daugherty fixed her in advance?

First appeared in somewhat different form in *The New York Review of Books*, March 29, 1990.

Madame Marcia duly foresees the presidency in the stars and rampant lion of the horoscope. But she also sees a darker fate. In answer to the question: "He'll die?" she replies:

"We all do that. No. I see something far more terrible than mere death." Madame Marcia discarded her toothpick like an empress letting go her sceptre. "President Harding—of course I know exactly who he is—will be murdered."

We are now in the world of Gore Vidal. Many years ago, although an avid reader of his novels, I was uneasy in some parts of that world. I remember waxing a bit hot under the collar, reading *Burr*, at what I considered a travesty of the character of my hero, Thomas Jefferson. But since that time the bottom has fallen out of my old world. We have undergone Watergate and Irangate; we have seen a president resign from office under fire and a daydreaming movie star occupy the White House. If I hear the truth spoken by an elected official or his representative, I wonder if he has had no inducement to lie. I have had to face the nasty fact that the world is—and probably always was—a good deal closer to the one so brilliantly savaged by Vidal than any that I had fondly imagined.

And finally, in the second volume of Robert Caro's heavily documented life of LBJ the author attempts to prove that that the lauded Texas liberal was the greatest and most unabashed rigger of elections in our political history. We may yet live to see Vidal branded a sentimentalist!

Vidal has said that *Hollywood* is the last (though not

the last chronologically) of a sequence of novels loosely called his History of the United States, starting with *Burr*, which deals with Aaron Burr's conspiracy, jumping forward to *Lincoln* and the Civil War, pausing in *1876* to cover the scandal of the Hayes-Tilden election, then moving in *Empire* to the imperialism of Theodore Roosevelt, and ending in *Washington, DC*, with Joe McCarthy's reign of terror. *Hollywood* fills in the First World War and the Harding administration. But if the novels are all stars, at least in the brightness of their dialogue and character delineation, they do not form a true constellation. I doubt that they were really conceived as such before the writing of *Lincoln*. I find a true unit only in the trilogy of *Lincoln*, *Empire*, and *Hollywood*, which relate the grim, dramatic story of the forging, for a good deal worse than better, according to Vidal, of the American empire and its ultimate conversion into the celluloid of the moving picture, which is all he deems it to be worth.

In *Lincoln* he finds the only man in his epic to whom he is willing to concede true greatness. His portrait of his man raises the novel a head above the others of the trilogy and may even make it a significant addition to the mountain of books on the emancipator, many of which, in Vidal's opinion, are packed with lies. His Lincoln is not so much concerned with freeing the slaves; he wants to save the union in order to turn it into a huge, world-dominating state, the "empire" that will be the subject of the next two novels. The book ends with John Hay musing on the question of whether the assassinated president might not have willed his own murder "as a form of atonement for the great and terrible thing that he had done by giving so bloody and absolute a rebirth to his nation."

Henry James maintained that a great work of art must have a subject matter of some moral worth, and he did not hesitate to judge Flaubert's trivial and self-centered Emma Bovary as inadequate raw material for a serious novel. Without agreeing with him on the negative aspect of the question, one may admit that the character of the sixteenth president, which irradiates Vidal's novel, gives it a unique importance in the author's oeuvre. But it is still Vidal's skill that has woven history with the thread of his own imagination to create a protagonist as vivid as the subject of Sandburg's biography. The reader is credited with some acquaintance with the Lincoln legend so that the author has only to suggest his famous habit of storytelling, as in this description of the exhausted president rising from a sickbed to attend doggedly to the grim business of war:

> "Gentlemen." In the doorway stood the President. The clothes hung from him as if they contained not flesh but a wooden framework. The cords in the neck were like ropes. The face was sallow and sunken. But the eyes were cheerful and alert. "I have risen, as the preacher said when he left the widow's house."

Lincoln, unlike the other characters, is never seen from within (at least until the night before his assassination) but his exterior is sharp and clear. We see how he moves, yawns, stretches, stares, droops an eye in what might be a wink, raises his voice to a sharp crack or lowers it to a mutter, and we learn to deduce from his man-

ner how carefully he is balancing his own shrewd assessment of a dangerous interlocutor with the latter's inflat-
ed concept of his own political clout. We learn also how
skillfully he shields his own suspicions and deductions
behind a mask of self-deprecating comradery or even
buffoonery, and yet how splendidly capable he still is, at
chosen moments, of showing a steely will, an imposing
dignity. Lincoln knew how to seem naïve when he was
at his most subtle; he was never really at his ease, even
when he appeared to be almost too much so.

Nor does Vidal hesitate to show the president's startling ignorance of technical matters or the genuine
naïveté of some of his most cherished schemes. Lincoln
was surprised to learn that the Secretary of the Treasury
did not have to sign personally every greenback issued,
and he could never be persuaded that it would not be
practical to ship three and a half million blacks to a new
colony in Africa. But what did this matter in the high
light of his all important mission to save the Union? He
was never in the least ashamed of his frankly admitted
deficiencies. It was as if Christ had been been found
ignorant of some aspect of Roman law or of the intrica-
cies of the imperial succession.

If Vidal admires Lincoln as a force, he does not much
admire what that force created. The indissoluble Union
(and even today, in 1994, the United States is one of the
very few nations on the globe no part of whose conti-
nental entity has ever so much as suggested secession),
secured at the price of 600,000 lives, seems to the author
of *Empire*, the sequal to *Lincoln*, to have become the
plaything of windy politicians and yellow journalists.

Empire is set in the last days of McKinley's administration and in Theodore Roosevelt's first term. As in *Lincoln* almost all individuals of the era with any political, military, financial, journalistic, or social importance make their appearance, exposing themselves to the bleak comments of Secretary of State John Hay or of his pessimist best friend, the historian and world observer Henry Adams. The latter is almost as well characterized as Lincoln. It might be Adams himself talking when he compares senators in Washington to cardinals in Renaissance Rome:

> "You can't avoid them. That's why I flee to the twelfth century where there were only three classes of people: the priest, the warrior and the artist. Then the commercial sort took over, the money lenders, the parasites. They create nothing, and they enslave everyone."

But whereas *Lincoln* is peopled almost entirely with real persons, Vidal returns in *Empire* to the Burr-Schuyler-Sanford fictional clan of the earlier historical novels. Caroline Sanford and her half-brother, Blaise, contribute their cool charm, brilliant witticisms, and sexual expertise amusingly to the story, but they do not significantly assist their creator in his determined pursuit of a a reason for the decline and fall of American civilization, which is the real business of the trilogy.

Henry Adams wrote *Mont St. Michel and Chartres* as a study of twelfth-century unity, and *The Education of Henry Adams* as a demonstration of twentieth-century multiplicity. Worship of the Virgin had been the source of the great energy that had covered Europe with churches; seven hundred years later that energy was spending itself in chaos. Lincoln plays the role of the Virgin in Vidal's trilogy; his removal abandons his reunited nation to false gods. Indeed, the election of Ronald Reagan and the triumph of Hollywood, purveyor of fantasies to a dazed multitude, might be the last chapter in the education of Gore Vidal.

Caroline Sanford asks Del Hay, a son of John, if the Spaniards have really blown up the *Maine*. He replies: "Probably not, according to Father. But it's the way things are made to look that matters now." Caroline takes this very much to heart. Indeed, she bases her whole life on it. She concludes that power is "the only thing worth having in this democracy of ours" and that "the ultimate power is not to preside in a white house, or open a parliament while sitting on a throne, but to reinvent the world for everyone by giving them the dreams you wanted them to dream."

Elihu Root, McKinley's Secretary of War, translates this sentiment, in Vidal's most brilliant prose, in a stern lecture to Theodore Roosevelt, then governor of New York, but too openly avid to be nominated over the president in the approaching Republican convention.

"I take it for granted that you *must* be president one day. But today is not the day, or even tomorrow, because of your passion for the word 'reform.' On the other hand, the day that you cease to use that terrible word, so revolting to every good American, you will find that the glittering thing will drop—like heavenly manna—into your waiting lap. But for now we live in the age of McKinley. He has given us an empire.... You say unpleasant things about arrogant corporations, whose

legal counsel I happen to be. And I thrill at your fierce
words. . . . Oh, Theodore, you are a cornucopia of lovely
things! But McKinley has given us half the islands of
the Pacific and nearly all the islands of the Caribbean.
No governor of New York can compete with that.
McKinley, working closely with his God, has made us
great. Your time will come but not as vice-president to
so great a man. It is also too soon to remove yourself
from the active life of strenuous reformation, not to
mention the vivacious slaughter of animals."

This Root would have agreed with Vidal's maxim: "To
betray without cynicism is the mark of the master politi-
cian."

The novel ends with a tense private dialogue between
Roosevelt (now president) and William Randolph Hearst.
The two met in fact in 1905, but their talk was not recorded, and Vidal has reconstructed it from his always vivid
imagination. Hearst tells TR that he has "created" him by
making an heroic epic out of a small raid up a Cuban hill
and that he has forced him to invoke the Sherman Act
against the Oil Trust by revealing to the public that the
Trust financed TR's bid for a second term. Roosevelt
replies with as much dignity as he can muster that "true
history" will be the judge of both, to which Hearst retorts:
"True history is the final fiction."

Blaise and Caroline Sanford, who continue the saga in
Hollywood, have settled an old family feud by agreeing to
co-manage a Washington newspaper of wide circulation
and great political importance. They have a genealogical
connection with Charles Schermerhorn Schuyler, the
narrator of *Burr* and *1876*, who dies at the end of the

eponymous year, which is worthy of a Jacobean tragedian. Schuyler's daughter Emma, widow of the French Prince d'Agrigente, has plotted to marry the wealthy Colonel William Sanford after his wife has died giving birth to a child whose conception Emma knows will be fatal to her but which she has nonetheless wickedly encouraged. Mrs. Sanford duly dies giving birth to Blaise, and the next year Emma, now her successor, is justly punished by expiring at the birth of her own child, Caroline. The two babies are given a genetic head start to face the rigors of life in a Vidalian world.

Their creator has chosen the appropriate interpreters for his cool and unsentimental story. They are dedicated sophisticates, devoid of any prejudice and of any religious or even political bias, brilliant, charming, and quite as decent to others as others are to them, with wit, delightful manners, and a fixed determination to do anything they choose to do as well as it can be done. Above all, they aim to see the world as it is, no matter what conclusion that vision may entail. Caroline has been married to and divorced from a Sanford cousin, but her dismal, right-wing, Red-baiting daughter and only child, whom she understandably dislikes, is the child of a former lover, U.S. Senator Burden Day, another detached interpreter of the political scene. Sex in Vidalian fiction rarely gets out of hand. It is entirely physical, entirely for pleasure, and is indulged in with both sexes. Oddly enough, it is just the opposite of what it is in Proust, whom Vidal deeply admires, where it is identified with pain. Caroline's brother Blaise, who is married to an heiress, has a brief homosexual encounter in Paris with a *poilu* turned prostitute, an episode that might be deemed the trademark of a Vidal novel, like the foxhunt in Trollope or the appearance of Hitchcock as an extra in each of his films.

Caroline takes leave of the Sanford-owned newspaper to explore the new phenomenon of Hollywood in 1917, where she becomes not only the mistress of a director, Tim Farrell, but the leading lady of his films, under the name of Emma Traxler. That a middle-aged, world-famous newspaperwoman should become a movie star without anyone recognizing her surely lacks verisimilitude, but in the dreamlike reality that Vidal so successfully evokes we are only too happy to accept it. Blaise remains, for the most part, in Washington, which allows the reader to follow two of the three themes of the novel: the involvement of America in war and the rise of Hollywood to world power, each through the eyes of a Sanford. The third theme, the why and wherefore of the election of Warren Gamaliel Harding, we follow through the mind of one of his crooked henchmen, Jesse Smith.

The Sanfords, of course, know everybody. Caroline fills us in on Hearst, Marion Davies, Elinor Glyn, Douglas Fairbanks, Mary Pickford, the murdered William Desmond Taylor, and hosts of others, while Blaise introduces us to everyone of note in the capital from President Wilson down. It is an entrancing gallery of portraits, as funny as it is acute.

Wilson is the best, "an odd combination of college professor unused to being contradicted in a world that he took to be his classroom and of Presbyterian pastor unable to question that divine truth which inspired him at all times." Eleanor Roosevelt, then wife of the Assistant Secretary of the Navy, is "the Lucrezia Borgia of Washington—none survived her table." The malice of her cousin Alice Longworth, TR's daughter, has "the same sort of joyous generalized spontaneity as did her father's hypocrisy." As it was an article of faith that the American public could not fall in love with a screen star who was married in real life, Francis X. Bushman, the father of five, is "obliged to pretend to be a virtuous bachelor, living alone, waiting wistfully for Miss Right to leap from the darkened audience onto the bright screen to share with him the glamour of his life."

We see Wilson on board the S.S. *George Washington*, confiding to Blaise that he could have done well in vaudeville, and, to prove it, letting his face go slack and his body droop as he performs a kind of scarecrow dance across the deck singing: "I'm Dopey Dan, and I'm married to Midnight Mary." We see Charlie Chaplin and Douglas Fairbanks naked in a steam room discussing how they should have used some of their surplus earnings to buy the press and bury such Hollywood-damaging scandals as the Fatty Arbuckle affair. We see Mrs. Harding hurling furniture at her husband's mistress and Alice Longworth doing handsprings before her father's admirers.

Whether we believe it all or not, it is always in character, always more than possible. When a character suggests that a woman as plain as Eleanor Roosevelt would never have hired as her secretary as beautiful a woman as Lucy Mercer to be brought in constant contact with her handsome husband unless she had been attracted to her herself, one's first reaction may be one of shocked indignation, but then, when one pauses to consider it. . . . It is always that way with Vidal.

There are moments when a gathering of his characters takes on some of the features of a fancy dress party. One tries to identify each newcomer before he is introduced. Sometimes the characters are not. I think I spotted Rudolph Valentino in the young extra in a Hearst private movie who had "a square crude face" and eyebrows that grew together in a straight line "like those of an archaic Minoan athlete."

Through conversations with the capital's power wielders Blaise and Senator Day follow the slow enmeshing of a peace-loving president in the imbroglio of European war. "I do believe the Germans must be the stupidest people on earth," Wilson groans as the submarine sinkings mount. But he is helpless against the U-boat and Allied propaganda, as he will be helpless against the Republican Senate majority to save his league. Vidal sees our involvement in the war of empires as a mistake and one that cost us essential liberties in the Red-baiting era that followed, but he does not see how the mistake could have been avoided. America in his view, ever since Lincoln forged his new union, had been ineluctably committed to the course of empire. Empires are not good things; they ruthlessly exploit weaker tribes, but at least in Europe, with its aristocratic traditions, the process is carried out to its inevitable dissolution with a certain style. America, on the other hand, being a mix of peasant emigrations, is easily victimized by any sort of propaganda and doomed to make an imperial fool of itself.

Caroline, the author's primary spokesman, believes, like her mentor Henry Adams, in nothing but "the prevailing fact of force in human affairs." In Washington, where the game of force is played for its own sake and where morality is always relative to need, "one man's Gethsemane might be another's Coney Island." In Hollywood she finds things even worse.

Now the Administration had invited Caroline herself to bully the movie business into creating ever more simplistic rationales of what she had come, privately, despite her French bias, to think of as the pointless war. Nevertheless, she was astonished that someone had actually gone to prison for making a film. Where was the much-worshipped Constitution in all of this? Or was it never more than a document to be used by the country's rulers when it suited them and otherwise ignored?

She finds a new source of national power in the movies and begins to wonder if Hollywood might not even be able to persuade a defeated country that its army had been victorious, at least abroad.

A moving picture was, to begin with, a picture of something that had really happened. She had really clubbed a French actor with a wooden crucifix on a certain day and at a certain time and now there existed, presumably forever, a record of that stirring event. But Caroline Sanford was not the person millions of people had watched in that ruined French church. They had watched the fictitious Emma Traxler impersonate Madeleine Giroux, a Franco-American mother, as she picked up a crucifix that looked to be metal but was not and struck a French actor impersonating a German officer in a ruined French church that was actually a stage-set in Santa Monica. The audience knew, of course, that the story was made up as they knew that stage plays were imitations of life, but the fact that an entire story could so surround them as a moving picture did and so, literally, inhabit their dreams, both waking and sleeping, made for another reality parallel to the one they lived in. . . . Reality could now be entirely invented and history revised. Suddenly, she knew what God must have felt when he gazed upon chaos, with nothing but himself upon his mind.

She finds the war unpopular in California until the people succumb to every "anti-German, anti-Red, anti-negro demagogue," and she resolves, when peace comes, to use the new power of the film to offset some of the damage done. Whether she will enjoy success in her project is far from clear at the end of her tale.

The parts of the novel that deal with the handsome and amiable Warren Harding and the gang of crooks with whom he is too easygoing not to associate are highly amusing, but on a lower level. They are like the play put on by the mechanicals in *A Midsummer Night's Dream*, though considerably more ominous. Harding is shown as shrewd enough to see that if he is every delegation's second choice he will be nominated in a convention deadlocked over bigger men. I suppose the reason his story lacks the impact of the two other themes of the novel is that here Vidal has little to bring to our already settled conviction of its sordidness. He adds a murder or so for zest, but it is not essential. We know those men would have been capable of anything. (Very incidentally, speaking of murder, Vidal's solution of the famous one of the Hollywood director William

Desmond Taylor has been rebutted, at least so far as this reviewer's jury is concerned, by Robert Giroux's study of the subject, *A Deed of Death.*)

In *Hollywood*, as in many of Vidal's novels (*Lincoln* and *Julian* excepted), the parts are greater than the whole. But that is what he would say of the universe. In a senseless mosaic are not the beautiful details all the more precious? His highly polished prose style, in part the fruit of his classical training, is a constant delight. One might even go so far as to call him a modern La Rochefoucauld. I suppose it is a mistake to take sentences out of context to illustrate this, but I submit a few.

The Irish lover of a society girl "had entered her life like a sudden high wind at a Newport picnic, and everything was in a state of disorder."

Wilson, asked what was the worst thing about being president, replies: "All day long people tell you things that you already know, and you must act as if you were hearing their news for the first time."

And here is the end of the court of Henry Adams:

In the twenty years that Caroline had known Adams, neither the beautiful room, with its small Adams-scale furniture, nor its owner had much changed; only many of the occupants of the chairs were gone, either through death, like John and Clara Hay, joint builders of this double Romanesque palace in Lafayette Park, or through removal to Europe, like Lizzie Cameron, beloved by Adams, now in the high summer of her days, furiously courting young poets in the green spring of theirs.

Remembering
Marguerite Yourcenar

❧

When I was seated by Marguerite Yourcenar at a dinner given in her honor in New York—the occasion of her receiving the medal of the Commander of the French Legion of Honor and the National Arts Club's Medal of Honor for Literature—I placed before her my copy of *Memoirs of Hadrian*, which she had previously agreed to autograph. She had evidently already considered what she would write in it, for she rapidly inscribed her approval of this "good" first edition, the only one not marred by misprints. She then appended in solid capitals the words "LIBERTAS, HUMANITAS, FELICITAS," the motto engraved on Hadrian's coins. Thus moving from the exactly rendered particular to the broader universal, she put me in mind, however irreverently, of the lady with the squint in the Edward Lear limerick who "Could scan the whole sky /

First appeared in somewhat different form in *The New York Times Book Review*, January 11, 1988.

With her uppermost eye / While the other was reading small print."

Mme. Yourcenar, who died at eighty-four on December 17, 1987, had a small enough literary output for so long a life, but reading it is apt to produce the extravagant reaction that she knew all there was to know. Somehow the term "historical novel" does not fit her work. She moves so easily and confidently in time and space that a second-century Roman emperor, a sixteenth-century Flemish philosopher, or an anti-Communist combatant in post–World War I Lithuania seems as familiar as Vietnam veterans or antinuclear demonstrators. It is as if Yourcenar, orbiting in space, could plummet down into any country in any era and find herself at home. To her it really was one world.

So intent was she on the precise detail that when she lacked the restricting frame of a planned fiction, as she did in writing her autobiography, the facts almost ran away with her. Vivid and fascinating as these volumes are, one is not surprised that her story remained unfinished at her death. A hundred pages were needed for her ancestry alone; hundreds more for her childhood. But in her novels and tales, the strictest order prevailed, and some of the latter she was revising fifty years after their appearance.

I had originally planned to speak that night at the National Arts Club dinner on the subject of power in her fiction, and it was just as well that I decided to change my theme, as I should otherwise have given a touch of anticlimax to the eloquent address on just that subject with which the French ambassador to the United States, Emmanuel de Margerie, concluded the evening's ceremonies. He pointed out that in an age when writers of fiction dealt largely with the inner self, Yourcenar was one of the few who had treated in depth man's use of power over his fellow men.

I had been an admirer of Mme. Yourcenar's books ever since my college days, when *Alexis* stood out in a literature that still dealt rarely enough with homosexuality. It seemed, however, to me that the story was less concerned with its ostensible subject than with the broader one of love, just as those of her tales that treat historical events are more truly concerned with an ageless humanity. This universal quality in her work, this viewing of men as units of an organized society as well as introspective or neurotic individuals, draws her attention almost inevitably to problems of governance and the effect of rule on those who must impose it. I found myself particularly interested in the three novels that deal most explicitly with this theme: *Coup de Grâce, The Abyss,* and *Memoirs of Hadrian.*

Although I did not meet Mme. Yourcenar until the night of the National Arts Club party, I had corresponded with her the year before to choose a day on which I might call during a visit that I was planning to Northeast Harbor, Maine. It always struck me as a bit incongruous that this great Gallic savant should have chosen to reside on the Maine coast, but I imagined that she lived more on the wild and beautiful island that Champlain, discovering it in 1604, had named l'Île des Monts Déserts (the Isle of Bare Hills) than she did in the fashionable spa it has since become. At any rate, a meeting could not be arranged, for she had just been elected to the French Academy—the first female "immortal"—and her pretty cottage was being turned inside out as the setting for a television documentary. She protested on the telephone of her inability to receive a single guest; she was enmeshed, a modern Laocoön, in wires. But she was kind enough to say that what I had written her had taught her something about her work. I was too elated to care whether this were only what Henry James (whose *What Maisie Knew* Yourcenar has brilliantly translated into French) termed "the mere twaddle of graciousness."

The three novels that I see as dealing with power move progressively into the past.

In *Coup de Grâce*, set in the cold, foggy winter countryside of wartorn Lithuania, the power of life and death is given indiscriminately to individuals and groups fighting savagely and pointlessly in the aftermath of Armageddon. The eerie effect of her prose, praised by survivors of the civil conflict, is the more extraordinary in that she was not present in Lithuania in the years immediately following World War I. Her accomplishment is like that of Stephen Crane in *The Red Badge of Courage* or Stendhal's in the Waterloo chapters of *The Charterhouse of Parma*. And I know of no more shocking passage in modern fiction than the one in which the narrator is obliged to shoot with his own revolver the woman captive who has been his mistress. It is the ultimate madness of power in a world gone mad.

Moving back in time to sixteenth-century Flanders and Germany in *The Abyss*, Yourcenar transports us to a world that is only half-mad, for her hero philosopher is a priest of the life of reason who makes a gallant struggle to win the minds of his fellows before he perishes, the victim of a bigoted and superstitious Church. As *Coup de Grâce* is set in an atmosphere of misty cold, *The Abyss* is shrouded in a darkness lighted by the golden glints of Flemish palaces and the fire of the Inquisition.

Ironically, it is in her furthest penetration of the past that Yourcenar finds human reason at its strongest and clearest. *Memoirs of Hadrian*, her greatest novel, is cast in the form of a memorial written by the dying emperor to his ultimate heir, Marcus Aurelius, to guide him in his destiny of ruling the world and to warn him of some of his predecessor's errors. The eloquence and splendor of the style are in keeping with what the imperial philosopher might have written himself, and the supposed monograph is not interrupted by unlikely recollected dialogues or dramatically reenacted episodes. One can enjoy the illusion of reading a recently unearthed historical document.

To my mind the greatest achievement of what she called her "meditation upon history" lies in the sense conveyed of the essential loneliness of the man who has gained the supreme power and learned to use it humanely. It is a loneliness that his situation thrusts on him, but it is also a condition that he seems to need and almost desire. He cannot bear to be dominated by another human, and he comes to fear that even love will threaten his necessary independence. When love does bind him, toward the end of his reign, it is almost in nonhuman form. Antinoüs, the beautiful, muscular boy, silent, sultry, and utterly adoring, seems more like a faithful hound, and when he drowns himself in the belief that his sacrifice will prolong his master's life, it is as if he finally isolated Hadrian from the rest of humanity, condemning him to the solitude of the leader who has had the hubris to emulate a god.

Here is the beautiful passage describing the emperor's resistance to his passion for Antinoüs, his obsessive need to persuade himself that the Bythinian boy's selfless desire to please him smacks of the cringing seductiveness of the Roman women who had aspired to the imperial bed:

I was beginning to realize that our observances of that heroic code which Greece had built around the attachment of a mature man for a younger companion is often no more to us than hypocrisy and pretence. More sensitive to Rome's prejudices than I was aware, I recalled that although they grant sensuality a role they see only shameful folly in love; I was again seized by my mania for avoiding exclusive dependence on any one being. Shortcomings that were merely those of youth, and as such were inseparable from my choice, began to exasperate me. In this passion of a wholly different order I was finally reinstating all that had irritated me in my Roman mistresses: perfumes, elaborate attire, and the cool luxury of jewels took their place again in my life. Fears almost without justification had entered that brooding heart; I had seen the boy anxious at the thought of soon becoming nineteen. Dangerous whims and sudden anger shaking the Medusa-like curls above that stubborn brow alternated with a melancholy which was close to stupor, and with a gentleness more and more broken. Once I struck him; I shall remember forever those horrified eyes. But the offended idol remained an idol, and my expiatory sacrifices began.

The Two Marcels
of Proust

❧

The critic Percy Lubbock, in *The Craft of Fiction*, makes the point, sufficiently obvious today but much less so in 1921, that a lack of artistic organization in even a great novel, which may be concealed by brilliance of style or of characterization on a first reading, will become more apparent on subsequent visitations and may at least seriously diminish the reader's pleasure. Lubbock was particularly concerned with how the novelist handled his "point of view," that is, the way his story was apprehended by the reader, and he considered James and Flaubert the masters of this technique and Tolstoy a lax practitioner. The last time I reread *Remembrance of Things Past*, in the splendid C. Scott Moncrieff and Terence Kilmartin translation, I found myself wishing that Lubbock had included Proust in his study because, for the first time, I was conscious of a flaw

First appeared in *The New York Times Book Review*, August 4, 1985.

in that great work that seemed attributable to a confusion in the point of view from which the story is told. It was not, certainly, due to any laxness on the author's part. Proust gave the greatest care and attention to developing his narrator; the trouble was that no single point of view could quite perform the mammoth task required. The principal thesis of the novel is that a man's salvation consists in rescuing his past from the clutches of time, and the artist must show how this is done. If, however, he tells the story of his own past and how he recaptured it, his book may be as dull as a family photograph album. Proust elected to tell his story from the viewpoint of a fictional first person, a narrator who is only to some extent himself. The trouble lay in the definition of that extent.

There were immediate obvious problems. How could his "I" know, for example, in all its intimate details, the story of Swann's love affair with Odette, which took place before the narrator's birth? The reader has to accept the explanation that "I" was told about it; *Swann in Love*, as one critic put it, emulates the independence of a Romanesque chapel in a Gothic cathedral. More troublesome is the narrator's nosiness in spying on the lovemaking of Charlus and Jupien by climbing a ladder to peer through a transom window. Edith Wharton was particularly offended by this: "There is one deplorable page where the hero and narrator, with whose hypersensitiveness a hundred copious and exquisite passages have acquainted us, describes with complacence how he has deliberately hidden himself to spy on an unedifying scene."

But these are minor matters. My real difficulty lies not in what Proust's "I" sees, but in who he is. Nowhere in the novel is he given a name, except in *The Captive*, where he is called "Marcel," with the comment: "if we give him the same Christian name of the author of this book." This invites us to speculate that we may be dealing with a partial autobiography. If so, how seriously are we meant to take the narrator's claim that he is neither a snob nor a homosexual, when he is so obsessed with both and his author so obviously was both?

Let us take the snob first. Proust's alter ego is as tough on social climbers as Thackeray himself was. Yet he purports to see no taint of snobbery in being entranced with titles of nobility so long as they are associated with the history and landscape of France. Similarly, he sees no worldliness in a man's spending all of his evening hours at social gatherings so long as he is gleaning material for fiction. But no reader could miss the passion for society and all its trimmings that permeates Proust's lyrical descriptions of dinner parties and receptions. Would it not have been better to have built into his point of view that of the young society-obsessed social climber that Proust so obviously was? There is no reason that "Marcel" should not be candid about his enchantment with the aristocracy. I have no doubt Proust faced it in himself; he could have faced it in his puppet.

How else is one expected to react to this passage about "Marcel" in the little train on his way from Balbec to Doncière to visit Saint-Loup's army barracks? The narrator is studying a fellow passenger:

> The Lady wore an air of extreme dignity; and as I, for
> my part, was inwardly aware that I was invited, two days

hence, to the house of the celebrated Mme. Verdurin at the terminal point of the little railway line, that at an intermediate station I was awaited by Robert de Saint-Loup, and that a little further on I would have given great pleasure to Mme. de Cambremer by going to stay at Feterne, my eyes sparkled with irony as I gazed at this self-important lady who seemed to think that, because of her elaborate attire, the feathers in her hat, her *Revue des Deux Mondes*, she was a more considerable personage than myself.

Where is the irony? In which Marcel?

But a still greater difficulty was created by Proust's decision to make his narrator not only one of the few heterosexuals in the book, but one who regards inversion as a dangerous vice. This is not only inconsistent with the author's own life and philosophy; it does not really fit "Marcel's." It has often been pointed out that the narrator's affair with Albertine is credible only on the assumption that two males are involved, and many readers have found it drawn out and tedious. Proust told Gide that he dared not tell all. His lack of courage, however understandable in his day, cost him much of the verisimilitude of this part of his story. Contrast the plot he devised with the one he had to hand.

"Marcel" purports to fall in love with Albertine only after Dr. Cottard has pointed out to him that she and her girlfriend Andrée, while dancing together, are keeping their breasts in tight contact for mutual satisfaction. "Marcel" then proceeds virtually to imprison the young woman in his family's flat (the family being conveniently absent) to ensure her insulation from other tempting females. It is suggested that they do not have actual sexual intercourse, although Albertine is willing to lie naked in his arms. But despite the fact that "Marcel" suffers the tortures of the damned from jealousy on the rare occasions when he allows Albertine to go out alone, he refuses to buy emotional security at the price of marriage (which is presumably what the undowered Albertine wants) because he fears that she would soon bore him. Eventually she escapes and is killed in a riding accident. After a long time, "Marcel" gets over his grief.

Proust submits this neurotic case history as an ultimate revelation of the true nature of love. But suppose he had told the story, recounted in George Painter's biography of the author, of a rich bachelor and man about town who falls in love with his Italian chauffeur and is madly jealous of the latter's wife, who can give him a pleasure that his employer cannot? And suppose the chauffeur, a passionate worshiper of speed, insists on taking airplane lessons at his employer's expense, and is killed in a crash? Might this part of his novel not have gone beyond the case history to the universal?

Moreover, if "Marcel" were depicted as a homosexual, the reader would more readily accept his habit of regarding the whole world as homosexual. Many of the characters who are initially presented as exclusively heterosexual turn out to be homosexual as well in the course of the work: Legrandin, Odette, Gilberte, Saint-Loup. Others are more consistently homosexual: Jupien, Morel, the Prince de Guermantes, and, of course, Charlus. In the end the only characters who seem totally exempt from inversion are Swann, the Duc de Guermantes, and the narrator himself, who excoriates Charlus for attributing his own nature to others: "It was, indeed, exasperating to hear the whole world accused, and often without any semblance of proof, by someone who omitted himself from the special category to which one knew perfectly well that he belonged and in which he so readily included others."

A lesser flaw that springs from the confusion of "Marcel" with Proust is the prolixity of the work. I know it is heresy even to whisper it in academe, but I do not believe that *Remembrance* is tightly organized. Considerable passages are inserted almost in the manner of a journal. Some of the genealogies, the etymologies, the literary opinions are put in for no other reason than that they were of personal interest to the author. When the lift boy in Balbec tells the narrator that his sister has a habit of defecating in the backseats of hired cabs, surely this is simply something that struck Proust as novel. My only reason for mentioning such items is that they suggest that the work could be abridged—something not hitherto permitted by the holders of the copyright. Such an abridgement would bring Proust to many thousands of readers now put off by the formidable length of the work. I have little doubt that many of these would then reach for the full text, for *Remembrance* is certainly one of the greatest of novels. It might have been even greater had Proust seen fit to close the gap between the two Marcels.

Portrait of the Artist
as Strether

❧

I n a recent volume of essays, *Fiction and the Figures of Life*, William Gass suggests a difficulty for any biographer of Henry James. It is the possibility that the real psychic dramas in a life so exclusively literary may have lain, not in the events and emotions usually considered as the core of any writer's story, but in his struggle with words. What if James's mysterious accident on the fence in the fire in Newport, or the death of Minnie Temple, or the suicide of Constance Fenimore Woolson, or even the homoerotic friendship with the young Norwegian sculptor were minor episodes compared with his failure to write good plays or with the tortured development of his late style? Might Gass's idea not be the key to a different emphasis in the whole art of literary biography?

Did James perhaps have a sense of this himself? Did he realize that his heart, like his mind, was more dedi-

First appeared in *New Criterion*, June 1986.

cated to words than to people? This could explain his belief that a writer should not marry, a theory easily rebutted by the lives of countless authors who managed both to write and to marry well. It might also explain why he embraced his friends, in Gass's phrase, as though he were conferring degrees, why he made near parodies of his grave professions of affection, and why his correspondence is so larded with what he himself called "the mere twaddle of graciousness." He could have been making up for what he recognized as a lack of feeling, or at least a lack of the degree of feeling generally expected.

I can also find in this a clue to James's antagonism toward the idea of any biography of himself, and a clue to the great bonfire that he ultimately made of his private papers and correspondence. But what he did not destroy was the notebooks in which he recorded his relationship with his muse, the one consuming passion of his life. Hear him in 1910, at work on *The Ivory Tower*:

> Thus just these first little wavings of the oh so tremu-
> lously passionate little old wand (now!) make for me, I
> feel, a sort of promise of richness and beauty and vari-
> ety: a sort of portent of the happy presence of the ele-
> ments. . . . I seem to emerge from these recent bad days
> . . . and the prospect clears and flushes, and my poor old
> blest Genius pats me so admirably and lovingly on the
> back that I turn, screw round and bend my lips to pas-
> sionately, in my gratitude, kiss its hand.

He seems to be crooning to the muse that he sometimes addresses as "*caro mio*"; there is no language quite like it in his fiction or correspondence.

Although James's plots, even in the final phase, tend to verge on the melodramatic, there is one single exception, *The Ambassadors*, where the drama is largely confined to the mind of the reflector of the action: Strether. It occurred to me, after reading Gass's essay, that the character of Strether might have constituted a part of James's autobiography, or at least a statement of his artistic credo. Strether, in short, might be the one comment that he felt should be made about his own life as a writer.

Strether is like James in many ways: he is amiable, conservative, with the pleasantest manners in the world and the keenest sense of humor. He radiates kindness to an outward world with which he is never very closely engaged. His wife and little "dull" son are long dead, and the latter is more a source of guilt feeling than sorrow—he has not cared enough for the boy. Strether goes to Paris to carry out a mission imposed on him by a woman who is far stronger than he; he accepts the task out of passivity and duty. But once in Paris he discovers . . . well, simply everything: beauty, life, art, all that he has missed in the first fifty-five years of his existence. He is redeemed; he lives at last, but as an artist lives, in his own enlightenment. And nothing else really matters now, not because the affairs of other human beings are not important, but because they do not really want him to be concerned with their affairs. They wish, thank you very much, to take care of their affairs in their own way.

So the whole matter of detaching Chad Newsome from his French mistress and bringing him home to business and domesticity falls of its own weight. It no longer matters what Chad will do, since Chad will do it anyway; but in the meantime Strether has discovered what life—or at least his own life—is all about.

Strether in the end will return to Woolett, Massachusetts, but he will have no more influence on the lives of his friends there than he has had on those of his friends in Paris. Chad will probably marry Mamie Pocock; in any event, he will marry someone very like her. Mrs. Newsome, Chad's mother, will not become Mrs. Strether, but her life will be the same as it was before she considered that alternative. Aided by her nasty daughter, she will preside serenely over the small town's society. And in Paris Madame de Vionnet will be *triste* for a while over the loss of Chad, but she will be French and realistic and adaptable. Poor Maria Gostrey will be the only person to have been permanently affected by Strether, for she has loved him, but she, as James himself once said, is only a *ficelle*—a piece of string to hold the plot together—and how sorely can a *ficelle* suffer? I seem almost to make something out of the fact that only a *ficelle*, i.e., not a real person, could fall in love with James-Strether.

So the only person whose life *will* be changed is Strether himself. He will be a different man, a man with a vision, for his experience has turned him into an artist—after all, he has expressed to himself the whole novel that we have read—and as an artist he will stand apart from the others in a loneliness that presumably has its own compensating ecstasy.

Strether's vision came when he was fifty-five; James's own must have happened much earlier, probably when he gave up Harvard Law School with a deep relief to dedicate himself to letters. But in composing his plan for

The Ambassadors he could still have identified himself with the nonwriting Strether, musing on what might have been his fate in Woolett, possessed of an artist's imagination but of no art, as in *The Jolly Corner* he speculated on the man he might have become had he stayed in New York and gone into business. The early devotion of his own career to the craft of fiction did not exempt him from the trials of other mortals, but his greatest ones would come over the use of words.

Pater and Wilde

Aestheticism and Homosexuality

The pictures of Walter Pater (1839–1894) as a don at Brasenose College in Oxford that have come down to us from his contemporaries show little variation. We see clearly enough the high receding forehead and the bright, near-together eyes, the pale homely face and the moppy moustache, and we follow the ascetic, slightly stooped figure in its quick, shoulder-swinging walk from the lecture room or the chapel (where he would remain kneeling in the deepest reverence throughout the sacrament) to his two small chastely furnished rooms, painted in greenish white, their decor confined to three or four line engravings and a bowl of dried rose leaves. One thinks of his answer to a parlor game question of what animal he would have chosen to have been could he not have been human: "A carp swimming forever in the green waters of a royal château." Perhaps he had almost achieved it.

First appeared in somewhat different form in *New Criterion*, October 1991.

In these rooms he would receive with grave and patient kindness the students whose papers he would take to the window seat with a "Well, let us see what this is all about." And here in contented solitude he would compose the beautiful books and essays which would bring him ultimately the fame that was at times as agitating as it was dear.

All of which does not mean, of course, that Pater did not seethe inwardly, not only with the famous "hard gemlike flame" that he urged his readers to seek but with less ethereal fires. Indeed, his lyrical outbursts on the subject of naked male beauty seem positive indications of homosexual feeling, however repressed in his daily existence, and have been widely taken as such in our day.

Thomas Wright, whose startling two-volume biography of Pater appeared in 1907, attempted to show his subject as less inhibited than generally supposed. He had not known Pater himself, and the latter's two adoring if rather spectral maiden sisters had refused to help him, but Wright got hold of one Richard C. Jackson, a rich Oxford scholar who owned a large estate with a private chapel in Camberwell, where Pater, apparently a constant visitor, was able to wear "his heart upon his sleeve." Jackson, handsome, young, and devout, clad in the black garb of the Augustine canons and calling himself "Brother à Becket," provided Pater, according to Wright, not only with the great love of his life but with the model for Marius the Epicurean. Jackson had even boasted in verse to Pater:

> You greet me as your Marius! Me
> Who swelled for your life's minstrelsy in ivor towers.
> I say to thee,

Pater and Wilde

Within my garden I enclose
Your spirit with a damask rose
Of ivor towers.

Could the author of the famous rhapsody on Mona Lisa in *The Renaissance* have suffered this effusion without wincing? I think it possible. Jackson's naïve, emotionally charged, but perhaps chaste High Church group may have provided Pater with a haven where he could express his love for his handsome friend without the implications of sodomy that his Oxford world would surely have drawn and from which he himself may well have shrunk back in fear and dismay.

In *Marius the Epicurean* Pater found his true medium, which would be neither the essay nor fiction but a combination of both. The novel's hero, a deeply meditative aristocrat in the day of the later Antonines, the golden age when, according to Gibbon, the empire comprehended the fairest part of the earth and the most civilized portion of mankind, lives until the very end of his story a life almost entirely of the mind. For him, as with his creator, the temptations of the world do not come as a longing for love—to be with "Cynthia or Aspasia"—but as a thirst for an existence in exquisite places. Some of his youthful emotions may be directed toward the beautiful poet Flavian and toward the handsome but dispassionate centurion Cornelius, but his final goal is chastity, "the most beautiful thing in the world and the truest conservator of the creative energy." Here we may have Pater's own credo: never to mix together the flesh and the spirit or make the matter of a heavenly banquet serve for earthly meat or drink.

Women, of course, were not the danger. It was the couplings of men that Pater feared and detested, like the mating of the writhing snakes that so appalled his hero and that he may have associated with the lustful empress Faustina borne in her closed litter to the park where the athletes strip. Pater might have agreed with Arthur C. Benson, who described even the mild homoerotic gestures of affection offered by Henry James to younger men as "the slobbering osculations of elderly men with false teeth." Born with desires unacceptable to society and to himself, Pater attempted to sublimate them into his art.

It is difficult to write on this subject in our day of militantly defensive toleration without risking the imputation of prejudice, but I am concerned here not so much with the intolerance of the late-nineteenth-century British public toward homosexuals as with the effect of this attitude on the homosexuals themselves. Many, perhaps even most, like Pater, sensed a correspondence between the condemnation of the establishment and their own deep feelings of guilt. A. E. Housman, in the poem commencing "Shot so quick, so clean an ending?," counsels suicide as a brave man's worthiest solution to a felt attraction to his own sex: "You would not live to wrong your brothers; you died, lad, as befits a man." And yet we now know that Housman himself slipped furtively across the Channel to visit male brothels. Happily for British poetry, he did not take his own advice.

Theodore Roosevelt's elder daughter is thus quoted in *Mrs. L: Conversations with Alice Roosevelt Longworth*: "Wasn't it George V who is reputed to have said about a peer arrested for homosexuality, 'I thought men like that shot themselves.' Well, Father was a bit like that."

Pater's solution to the problem was chastity. Chastity is not held in high regard in our time, but we should remember that through history countless thousands of men and women have deemed it not only the surest path to a spiritual union with God, but a vital conserver of natural human energy. I suggest that Pater believed that abstention from all sexual acitivity would be of essential assistance to him in writing the most graceful and mellifluous prose of his day. And I have little doubt that Henry James harbored a similar notion. It was very likely a delusion, but I think it may have brought them both, from time to time at least, a peculiarly intense form of happiness and relief.

Oscar Wilde, of course, provides abundant evidence that chastity is not an indispensable handmaiden to the art of writing exquisite prose. Neither Pater nor James himself made finer use of the English language than the author of "The Decay of Lying," "The Critic as an Artist," *The Picture of Dorian Gray*, the four great comedies, and *De Profundis*. But it may have been the same sense of guilt that drove the others to a kind of literary monastery which impelled him to defy the gods, to spit in the eye of the devil in whom he half believed. I cannot read the terrible record of his trials without finding in them a species of compulsion, almost of suicide, however differently motivated from that of Housman's "lad."

The monk of old denied himself the pleasures of the flesh because he anticipated greater ones either in the ecstasy of mysticism or in a life hereafter, or in both.

Pater does not seem to have had such faith in a divine bestowal of these spiritual delights, but he yearned to develop it. His Marius as a young man has a brooding sense that he must train himself for some great occasion of self-devotion that should consecrate his life, as martyrdom stamps the seal of worth on a Christian's. And in the end of his tale this indeed comes, when he and Cornelius are arrested by soldiers on an anti-Christian raid, and he contrives his friend's release, himself remaining, on the plea of seeking counsel in Rome. Marius is not actually martyred; dying of fever and exhaustion on a forced march, he is left to expire on the roadside in the care of some country people who turn out to be Christians and who administer the last rites.

In the passages of Marius's last moments we learn first of his gratitude for the goodly vision with which his life has been blessed—one long unfolding of the beauty and energy of things. "*Vixi!*" he can indeed exclaim. But this is followed by his rueful sense of perhaps wasted powers, by the dismal apprehension that extinction will terminate a life that has been nothing but a passage of sweet music, from dying hour to dying hour, sufficient only to itself. And then he has a gleam of a Christian afterlife.

But only a gleam. We are not sure, as Marius succumbs amid the chants of "*Abi! Abi! Anima Christiana!,*" that his is quite that. The inference might even be drawn that he does not really wish anything to be substituted for a mind or soul that has dwelt so happily with beauty. Perhaps he is content to die with Keats's aphorism from "Ode on a Grecian Urn" on his lips. We may remember that Pater himself once wondered what sort of man would be willing to change the curve or color of a rose leaf for the colorless, formless, intangible being that Plato placed so high.

The eponymous hero of *Sebastian van Storck* may be even closer to his creator than Marius. This grave young Dutchman of the seventeenth century rejects all positive things, friends, family, riches, and the love of a fine woman, to brood instead over the thought of the earth under his feet cooling down forever from its old cosmic heat. Yet people love Sebastian; his intellectual melancholy, like Hamlet's, gives a bodily sweetness to all he says and does. Life to him is but the troublesome surface of the one absolute mind, a passing vexatious thought or uneasy dream, and he yearns to put aside the picturesque world of Dutch art and Dutch reality and die to self in an eternal nothingness that he likens to the dead level of a glacial and lonely sea under a pallid Arctic sky. In the end Sebastian is drowned in a beach house by a mammoth tide, but his last act is to save the life of a child, so, like Marius's, his story ends on a faint note of redemption and hope. But only a faint one. Never has a sense of beauty been more hauntingly identified with its very evanescence.

Wilde went in for robuster pleasures. As a youth he had hailed the sensuous Keats as his idol in poetry, and he had literally prostrated himself before the grave of the young bard in Rome. But he showed equal fervor for Pater, whom he deemed his master in what the latter had persuaded him was the more difficult literary form. "Pater," he proclaimed, "is the only man in the century who can write prose." The author of *Marius*, however, was made uneasy by the noisy adulation of this new disciple and complained of the "strange vulgarity" that Wilde regarded as his peculiar charm.

It seems likely that Pater feared that Wilde's public posturing and unabashed eulogizing of "Greek love" would bring down the wrath of the public on all who might be branded with the term "aesthete." For what to a Philistine was the difference between pederasty and aestheticism? And indeed after the conviction and jailing of Wilde, the chorus of the press would express the growl: "So *this* is what art makes of a man! We suspected as much!" Pater, at any rate, would escape all this, for he died prior to Wilde's suit against the marquis of Queensberry.

Certainly Wilde was nothing if not provocative. To amuse or even anger his lecture audiences he took deliberate advantage of the popularity of Gilbert and Sullivan's *Patience*, a parody of the aesthetic movement, to pose as a real-life Bunthorne and to exalt beauty for beauty's sake over drab middle-class morality and conventionalism. But the irony of his career was that he gained a more enduring eminence in the memory of men by the tragedy of his public disgrace than by all the seeming frivolity that preceded it, a frivolity that was often a mask to cover a deeper wit and philosophy.

But was it really ironic? Perhaps Wilde's fate was a willed one, the black final curtain intended to eclipse the froth of too many paradoxes. If Wilde stated on one occasion that he had made the trivial in thought and action the keystone of the philosophy expressed in his plays, he also wrote to Lord Alfred Douglas in *De Profundis*: "Nothing really at any period in my life was ever of the smallest importance compared with art." Was he not close to Pater here? And as he also insisted that he had tired of his hedonistic life with Douglas, his seemingly lunatic persistence in prosecuting Lord Queensberry for calling him, at least by implication, a homosexual, when he knew what incriminating evidence could be flung back at him by the defense, may have been a despairing need to endow with a dramatic seriousness a life at least open to the charge of inconsequence. He later went so far as to speculate that his friendship with Douglas may have been the prelude to what had been basically from the start a "symphony of sorrow, passing through its rhythmically-linked movements to its certain resolution, with that inevitableness that in Art characterizes the treatment of every great theme."

In this fashion, writing *after* the debacle, he was able to turn the whole sordid matter into a tragedy of Greek dimensions, obscuring in a Platonic eulogy the boy prostitutes, the bibulous parties in hotel brothels, and even the fecal stains on sheets produced as police evidence of sodomy. Think what Pater would have thought of the latter! But never mind. Wilde thus accomplished a remarkable feat in literary history: that of fusing his works with his biography, so that they seem to many readers a single work of art. One even wonders if either his writings or his purgatory would be quite so famous today without the assistance that each lends to the other.

"My dear blest Percy!"
Percy Lubbock and Edith Wharton

1

Percy Lubbock (1878–1965) had the perfect training, background, and intellectual equipment to become a major novelist of his time. Well-connected, a graduate of Eton and King's College, Cambridge, he had addressed himself early to the literary life, not only as a student and scholar but as a cultivator of older literary luminaries. While still a young man he became the intimate friend of Arthur Christopher Benson, Howard Sturgis, Henry James, and Edith Wharton. He would ultimately edit Benson's voluminous diaries and the letters and fiction of James, who apostrophized him in a letter as "my dear blest Percy!"

He not only started surely; he proceeded with care. His first book was a life in letters of Elizabeth Barrett Browning; his second, a short biography of Pepys, of

First appeared in somewhat different form in *New Criterion*, May 1985.

whose library in Magdalene College, Cambridge, he was for a time director. It was not until 1921 that he published *The Craft of Fiction* and made a name for himself by drawing up the "principia" of the modern novel and proclaiming James as its master practitioner. In the latter's late style he saw the perfect union of form and matter:

> The well-made book is the book in which the subject and the form coincide and are indistinguishable—the book in which the matter is all used up in the form, in which the form expresses all the matter. Where there is disagreement and conflict between the two, there is stuff that is superfluous or there is stuff that is wanting; the form of the book, as it stands before us, has failed to do justice to the idea.

From now on Lubbock's creative pace accelerated. The next year saw the appearance of *Earlham*, his nostalgic description of the ancestral Norfolk seat of his mother's family, the Gurneys. England's stately homes have been often and lovingly depicted in lacquered prose, but Lubbock's evocation of this ancient mansion, red and mellow, spacious, sunbathed, with gables of flint and brick and high-sashed windows, is perhaps the finest of all. George Lyttelton, writing to Rupert Hart-Davis in 1957, inquired: "Who was the good man I met recently who shared my opinion of *Earlham*, i.e., as a book of almost unique beauty? It is about the only thing of importance I am quite sure of."

Lubbock knew just what he was doing in *Earlham*; had he allowed it to become fiction, it would have been nothing. The reproduction of settings and personalities in luminous prose was to become his peculiar accomplishment, and he understood that in so doing he had to be accurate or lost:

> In telling an imaginary story a writer is content to leave the reader in his error. The reader imagines the house, the room, the garden, as he pleases; what matter if it is all distorted, rearranged, so long as certain few details are correctly placed? An old-fashioned room, a window-seat, some high-backed chairs, some portraits on the panelled walls—enough, there is a setting for the blush-tinted maiden who gazes from the window, a letter just falling from her hand. So the story might begin, and the author would contentedly leave you to fill in the picture of the room as you choose—with a thousand points of unlikeness to the room as he thought of it. But in a true story, like mine, everything seems to be spoilt if you deviate from my memory at any point—if you place, for example, the wrong kind of Chinese cups and beakers on the cabinet, if you omit the little cluster of humming-birds under their glass dome on the table, if you are confused on the subject of the green roses in the carpet.

Finally, in 1923, he made his first venture into fiction with the exquisite *Roman Pictures.* His narrator, a young man of the late 1890s, is determined to flush out the "real" Rome, and he soon abandons the lead of his more sophisticated friend, Deering, who purports to find it on the fringe of bohemia with fledgling actors and singers. The narrator's technique is simply to allow himself to drift from milieu to milieu, usually among expatriates or Italians with some foreign connection, since they are the persons most to hand. He explores the neighborhood of the Vatican, the atelier of a Romantic painter, a scholar's study, the Forum under the guidance of a professor, and finally the splendid salon of an intellectual English-born marchesa, the "real thing," if such still exists, only to meet there her nephew, who turns out to be . . . yes, Deering! E. M. Forster, in *Aspects of the Novel*, compared *Roman Pictures* with *The Ambassadors* as a perfect example of what he called the "great chain" plot.

Roman Pictures is fiction, but it is also the portrait of a city, and one feels that each of the characters is modeled upon someone whom Lubbock has observed. He did not have to know them well; a quip, a smile, a frown, a phrase, an attitude were all he needed to draw these wonderfully amusing caricatures for whom the fine pink glow of the Eternal City provides so vivid a background. Indeed, Rome is the principal character of the book. When the narrator sees and hears the great roaring crowd of pilgrims in St. Peter's, he wonders if a church can be the true temple of the Roman genius:

> It stands upon the hill of the Vatican in our day, and it has stood there for some little time; but its rightful place is the Capitol, the mount of triumph—it is there that the temple belongs. Kings and queens were led captive to that shrine, the multitude mocked and jeered at their abasement; and I see what is wanting to the due completeness of the resounding assembly in St. Peter's—it is the presence of captive kings and queens, brought low by the power of Rome, over whom the multitude might exult with glee and ferocity.

Lubbock had now set out the rules for the novel; he had mined the rich field of his childhood, and he had made his first experiment in fiction. He was ready for a major novel. All that he needed, at forty-five, was the right subject, and what did he have more precisely to hand than a young man's discipleship to a great artist? Like his own with Henry James?

The central theme of *The Region Cloud*, published in 1925, could indeed have sustained a Jamesian novel. It is the study of a fashionable and brilliant portrait painter, Channon, a monster of egotism, as seen through the eyes of his adoring but ultimately disillusioned secretary. Unfortunately, the protagonist turns into a straw man and a bore.

What is basically wrong with the novel is illustrated in the chapter where two critics, an academician and a modernist, visit Bintworth, Channon's great country estate, to study his work. The reader is thoroughly amused by their caustic reactions, vividly noted by the Lubbock of *Roman Pictures*, until the supposedly all-seeing secretary Austin says of them:

Such are the diversions of a watchful spectator at Bintworth; they are trivial, and it is just their triviality that fixes them in the memory. For when they pass and cease, and when Channon is alone with his work again, the tiny echo they leave on the spacious air is absurd.

But is it? Do we ever see Channon at work? We do not. Lubbock was simply unable to create a major character and to get inside of him. He had to work from models:

persons, mansions, schools, cities; his genius lay solely in literary painting. He might have created a great picture of Henry James at work; he could not do Channon.

It is tempting to speculate that Austin, the secretary-narrator, may take on a bit of the nature of Lubbock himself. In one scene he toys with the idea that the only superiority he could possibly claim over Channon might lie in the fact that he has *not* indulged in the inevitable vulgarity of a practiced art but has remained aloof and pure as the uncontaminated observer and critic. Channon may be worth a pound a minute—yes—but Austin knows that he's not worth a penny more. But if Lubbock allowed himself this private fantasy of a momentary advantage over the master, James, he was quick to quash it in the end when Channon's discarded mistress points out a resemblance between Channon and Austin. For that's it; they are *both* egotists!

Did Lubbock know that he had failed in *The Region Cloud*? We only know that in a long life he never wrote another word of fiction. The year after its publication he married a rich, brilliant, beautiful, hypochondriacal English wife, Lady Sybil Cuffe, moved into the Villa Medici in Fiesole, and spent much of his time taking care of her. When he published next, in 1929, it was to revert, happily and successfully, to a mood of nostalgia in *Shades of Eton*.

Lubbock's last book, in 1947, was *A Portrait of Edith Wharton*. Here he succeeds where he failed in *The Region Cloud*, for he does not have to invent his great artist; he has her. And his book is just what its title implies: a portrait. We see Edith Wharton always from the outside; we are warmed by her laughter, intrigued by her febrile activity, impressed by her perfectionism, awed by her rigorous standards, and chilled by her acerbity and hauteur. If Lubbock knew of her affair with Morton Fullerton—and he probably did—he saw no more need for it in his "portrait" than had he been actually limning her likeness.

2

Sufficient controversy was stirred up over the question of how good a likeness Lubbock's "portrait" of Edith Wharton was, to make this perhaps the most lasting of his books. Wharton's literary reputation has grown steadily in the 1980s and '90s until she is now generally regarded as one of the major figures in American letters. I attribute this to three reasons: first and foremost to her penetrating analysis of the mores of New York City's financial upper class, couched in hard, glittering prose and garnished with scathing wit; secondly, to the fact that that class is now enough in the past to have become history and no longer arouses the envy and resentment of the less privileged; and finally to the force of the feminist movement, the extremists of which seek to deify women of past accomplishment.

Much of what has been written of Wharton in recent years adheres faithfully to the legend of the thorny path of her coming of age. She is seen as the lonely child of a fashionable and uncaring mother who scorns her scribbling habits and gives her only discarded brown wrapping paper on which to compose her silly tales. Growing up she is forced into the straitjacket of a debutante's idle career, with no end but a loveless marriage to a socially eligible bachelor. It is not until her late thirties that she breaks at last through the confining walls of Philistia and escapes to freedom and Paris and the joys of creation, surrounded by her intellectual peers. This is the legend preferred by Wharton herself and more or less set forth in her memoirs, *A Backward Glance*, which some wag termed her finest novel.

But there is another version of her growth and development which may be truer and is certainly more interesting. A scholar named Mary Pitlick has devoted much of her adult life to the exhaustive research of Wharton's early years and has amassed such copious information about her family, her friends, and the whole New York and Newport social setting of that era that she has not as yet been able to reduce it to publishable form. I offer this one example of the depth of her probing. Every student of Wharton's life has encountered the persistent rumor (in my opinion a canard) that she was not the daughter of George Arthur Jones, but of his wife, Lucretia, and of an English tutor of the two older sons who was supposed to have later gone west and perished in Custer's Last Stand. The story was believed by at least one close friend of Wharton's, Mrs. Walter Gay, wife of the artist. No one, however, before Pitlick has been able to establish even the existence of the tutor. But she, by poring through unpublished letters and journals of the day, has discovered persons who had actually met the tutor when dining with the Joneses. Armed with his name she was able to reconstruct his life story and find that he had indeed gone west and been killed by Indians, though not at

Little Bighorn. Pitlick has not so far been able to place him in Mrs. Jones's bed, nor do I think she ever will. But it is interesting to know that he actually existed.

The Edith Wharton that emerges from Pitlick's as yet uncompleted studies is a much stronger character than the one popularly imagined and sits well for Lubbock's portrait. This Edith thoroughly enjoyed the social life of her younger days; indeed, she was considered almost "fast" by some of the censorious. And far from being dominated by her mother, she made her willpower well known to her family. Not only did the Joneses not discourage her writing; they actually, when she was only sixteen, arranged for a private printing of her poems and distributed them to their friends. One recent critic, faced with this fact, sought to explain it away by arguing that the Joneses must have done this to humiliate their daughter! Yet in my precious copy of *Verses* (one of some dozen that survive) the young Edith Jones has inscribed it to her cousin, Edith Newbold, and carefully inked in her own corrections. She appears to have cheerfully cooperated with the generous action of her proud parents.

It appears, furthermore, that Edith was always free to read and write what she wanted, and if she produced very little in her twenties and early thirties there is no evidence that this was caused by her family's disapproval. I suppose it is always possible that the fashionable world's scant interest in literature may have deterred her, but I fail to see why it should have had this effect in her case any more than in the earlier one of Julia Ward Howe or the slightly later one of Amy

Lowell. The aggressively erudite young married woman whom Paul Bourget met in Newport in 1895 certainly showed no signs of being awed or repressed by the glittering summer colony of which she was a charter member. All her life she knew exactly what she wanted and usually got it, with the exception of her neurotic weakling of a husband whom she had at length to shed. She coveted a milieu of people with the good manners and proper deportment of society folk, but who at the same time should be cultivated, congenial, and stimulating, and she ultimately found it in Paris. Heavy drinking and obscene talk she would have none of in her salon, even if it entailed the elimination of genius.

Here is how the young Percy Lubbock first saw her in 1903 at the Windsor house of that brilliant and lovable, softly epicene and constantly knitting, middle-aged and wealthy bachelor Howard Sturgis:

> But she was a singular young woman. Though she was pleased with her place [position in the world], well content to keep and adorn it, and never had the least inclination to flout the law under which she was born, she was determined to have a great deal more than the mere portion prescribed to Edith Jones. Like a hungry young hawk, her mind was somehow to be fed; and she clutched at any sustenance within reach, wherever it appeared, tearing her way through it all with the passion to know, to see, to judge, which was her particular and private possession, never to be quenched or satisfied.

I cannot resist another quote from this same chapter because to me it almost guarantees the accuracy of

Percy Lubbock and Edith Wharton

Lubbock's observations of his group. In describing the attitudes of Henry James and of their host, Sturgis, toward Edith Wharton, he beautifully distinguishes between the elegant but perfunctory approval of the self-centered great artist and the deeper concern of the man who lives for his friends:

> Henry stooped and gathered her into his imagination with an Olympian benediction; Howard laid his possessions as a tribute at her feet; but which of the two stood entirely independent to observe her, ringing her round with the lightness of his irony, so clear and light that it could be taken for simple air? She knew all about it, no doubt; everyone knew that it was no more possible to dazzle Howard than to exhaust his indulgence; and for her, as for all of us, his place in friendship was ever a little apart from the rest, in a corner of his own—where nothing mattered but what you really were, and that was what he loved.

William R. Tyler, Edith Wharton's godson and perhaps the only person whom she loved both as a child and as an adult, had at first approved of Lubbock's *Portrait*, but rereading it twenty-five years later he was disagreeably struck by what he now saw as evidence of Lubbock's concealed dislike of his godmother. His reevaluation persuaded many readers to disregard it as a work of personal malice. Yet Lubbock himself, when asked if there was not some latent hostility in his portrait, beat his forehead and cried: "But I *adored* her!"
I believe that he did.

3

The story of Lubbock's long and intimate friendship with Edith Wharton, its sad breakup, and his decision, after her death in 1937, to paint a literary portrait of her from his memories of happier times is told in his letters (now in the Beineke Library at Yale) to his closest male friend, Gaillard Lapsley, who was also a friend of Wharton's. Lapsley was a staunch member of Wharton's little group of aesthetic bachelors, an American scholar of medieval history, "more English than the English," as R. W. B. Lewis has put it, and a member of the faculty of Trinity College, Cambridge. He would eventually become Wharton's literary executor and assist Lubbock in gathering material for the "portrait." My memory of Lapsley dates only from his old age; I recall his testily complaining to a waiter in a New York club that his toast had not, as requested, been buttered "on both sides" and sniffing that the moral beauty of Wharton's novels could never be appreciated by a sexually permissive society. I had marveled that Henry James could have ever apostrophized him as "my dear, dear boy." But I reminded myself that this crusty survivor of an age of titans had been taken very seriously indeed by the departed spirits.

Lubbock met Edith Wharton in 1909, when he was thirty and she was forty-seven. He sent Lapsley his first impressions:

> In the autumn I was here a good deal [Howard Sturgis's house in Windsor] and saw a good deal of Mrs. Wharton. What a woman—she rather terrifies me. I want people who will give me time—won't make up their minds

about me too quickly—won't let me see them "placing" me—don't you agree? Mrs. Wharton paralysed me by seeming to expect that I was going to be clever and intelligent all in a minute—it takes me at the best a long while! Long before my intelligence had time to act I felt my opportunity was gone. She is cleverer and more alive and finer than her books, I think. She has no business to be writing rotten little melodramatic anecdotes like the one I read in Scribner's yesterday ["The Bolted Door"]. Henry [James] turned up here several times while she was here—the moth to the candle—all beautifully himself he was.

Lubbock's initial reservations were quickly overcome, and he was soon able to tell Lapsley that Wharton was urging him "with characteristic beauty and bounty" to install himself, when he was dissatisfied with his temporary lodging in Vienna, for a couple of months in her apartment in the rue de Varenne and do his writing there. It is evident from the letters that Wharton was always tactfully aware of Lubbock's paucity of means (prior to his marriage), though he could never believe that she really knew how small they were. Her Paris invitation, however, he declined, as one of the pieces he was writing was, unbeknownst to her, about her books, and he could not quite see himself "sitting at one end of the flat writing about *her*, while she, at the other end, was writing herself."

He and Lapsley now began to refer to her as "the angel." The term was not wholly complimentary: Henry James, who set the tone for the group, used it first with a qualification, "angel of devastation," to describe

Wharton's rushing him off on wonderful excursions at the expense of his writing time. But Lubbock implied nothing but laudation when he informed Lapsley: "I have had archangelic letters from the angel in response to my stammering expressions of admiration and affection. *You* know I have been clinging to her and to you."

Lubbock's doubts about her bossiness, however, continued, and always would. She *was* bossy. In 1912 we find him highly critical of the way she tore James from "his hermitage, just when he had got settled to the silence and work he was craving for." "She has a nerve," he added. Lubbock was always keenly aware of the shortcomings of his nearest and dearest. It was what made him so astute and vivid a commentator on his early guide and mentor, Arthur Christopher Benson, whose massive diaries he edited. His love was never blind.

In the spring of 1914, with no foreboding of world disaster, Wharton and Lubbock took a motor trip (or "flight," as she liked to call it) through Algeria, all expenses paid by her. This marked the high point of their friendship. He wrote Lapsley that their parting after the excursion, even though they were to see each other daily in Florence, was "a cruel one" and that "it is hard to tell her what I think of her adorable goodness and affection and generosity, but I hope and think she understands my stammering accents."

Was there a hint here of warmer feelings? On either side? One rather doubts it. There were seventeen years between them. She had had only a single love affair in her life, according to Lewis, and that had ended unhappily four years before. And his reputation was that of a strict bachelor until his marriage, at forty-seven, to a woman of the same age.

The First World War, anyway, absorbed the energies of both—she with her hostels for refugees, he with the Red Cross in France and Egypt—and they met only on his rare passages through Paris. And there is some evidence that after the war Lubbock's recurrent depressions may have made him a less welcome guest. In 1922 Wharton wrote to Lapsley, after a visit Lubbock made to her château at Hyères on the Riviera:

> I think one of the reasons I didn't want to write was Percy. Has he said anything to you about his sojourn here? It was one of the most trying experiences I have ever undergone. His gloom was unrelieved, and he has simplified social life to the point of totally eliminating the feelings of others from his mind; he treated me and my other guests to six weeks of a morose and unbroken silence. Really and seriously, it was alarming—besides being very fatiguing. When he and I were alone it was no better, and so often, when one came into the room suddenly and he lifted that terrible *someone else's* face of which you once spoke, it gave me a chill.

Two years later, after another sojourn at Hyères, it was Lubbock who was complaining to Lapsley about his hostess:

> At Ste. Claire we had some days that were very delightful but that left me, to tell the truth, by no means without anxiety. The world is steadily more and more with her there—she was nearly worn out, that's the fact. . . . I

don't see what life of hers there is to shape except in the sense of tiring her out more and more. . . . I never saw her more worn or restless. How wrong it all is.

The end of the friendship came in 1926 with Lubbock's marriage to Lady Sybil Cuffe, daughter of an Irish peer, the earl of Dessart, who had been twice married, first to an American millionaire, Bayard Cutting, who had died young, and then to the English author of *The Architecture of Humanism*, Geoffrey Scott, whom she had divorced. Rich and popular, she held a kind of court for the Florentine international set in the magnificent Villa Medici in Fiesole. Actually it was Wharton who introduced Lubbock to Lady Sybil, never dreaming that the latter would want him for a spouse and acquire him, as rumor had it, by swooning in his arms when he accidentally dropped a lighted cigarette down the back of her dress.

Wharton expressed her candid opinion of this "insatiable female" in a letter to Lapsley about the sarcastically imagined danger to her bachelor court of Lubbock's defection: "It all makes me rather sick for him. This is the third of my friends she has annexed, and I see you and Robert [Norton] going next, and finally even Walter [Berry], kicking and screaming."

Iris Origo, daughter of Lady Sybil by her first husband, who remained, despite everything, a close friend of Wharton to the end, told me once when I was criticizing Wharton's possessive attitude about her circle of friends: "You must remember that Mother married, in quick succession, the three men whose friendship Edith most valued: my father, Geoffrey Scott, and Percy. It *was* rather hard."

Percy Lubbock and Edith Wharton

Lubbock discovered soon after his honeymoon in Ceylon that his wife's health was to be a permanent problem. She would live for seventeen more years, but as a semi-invalid, traveling in considerable state from villa to villa, from spa to spa, in a vain search for a lasting cure, lovingly attended and cared for by her devoted spouse. The hoped-for roses in his life were full of thorns. In 1927 he wrote Lapsley from Capri:

> And there is another sharp thorn which of course you know of—I can't talk to you without just mentioning it. Edith's tone to me—or to Sybil—or to both of us (for I don't understand—I am bewildered) has been and is a great pain to me. I don't begin to understand—it is so unnecessary—not to say so cruelly unjust. Well I have said what I can to her—it must wait. Basta.

But waiting made things no better between them. In 1933 a last effort was made by the Lubbocks to induce Wharton to come to the Villa Medici. She put an end to everything by sending word that she *might* be willing to overlook the past. Of course, the Lubbocks couldn't admit there was anything to overlook. Lubbock's last letter to Wharton is almost a wail:

> O Edith—you see *I* felt, seven years ago, as I still feel, that *you* might have thought you owed it to our old friendship and our many ties—not to say your still older and apparently friendly acquaintance with Sybil—to make sure you rightly and fairly understood what had happened—if there was anything in it that seemed wrong to you. And you wouldn't even try. You only made it clear that

Sybil was under your disapproval—and there you left her all these years. And now you are ready to "forget" the past. . . . I still hope for happier times.

They were not to come. But Lubbock saw in her death four years later, and in Lapsley's immediate suggestion that they work together on some kind of memorial book, the wonderful opportunity to bury old sores under a beautiful evocation of happier times. His friendship with Edith Wharton, after all, as he fully and gratefully acknowledged, had been one of the great things in his life, if not the greatest, for he had been much closer to her than to James. Her death, he wrote Lapsley,

> means to me the closure of so much—even though so much *had* been closed; or rather perhaps it means quite differently, the reopening of everything—of all the old days, and all the delight and the laughter and the charmed interest that was in them. Everything is with me again as I sit here this morning; you will understand how I need to talk of it with you—or rather to think of it with you, for it pours in from the past too abundantly, and too strangely and movingly, for talk just now.

It was agreed between him and Lapsley that he should write the book and that Lapsley would write all the friends for their reminiscences of Wharton. Both were slow if careful workers; the Second World War and Lady Sybil's death intervened, and it was ten years before *Portrait of Edith Wharton* appeared. It is, as has been already said, a portrait and not a definitive biography, but I believe it is necessary reading for students of American literature to amplify, qualify, and round out everything else that has been written about this remarkable woman and artist.

Tyler objects to Lubbock's picture of a woman who always insisted that her social status be recognized, who lived in a kind of regal state in houses that were too perfectly run to be quite comfortable, and who was capable of unkindnesses. But when I was young I knew many persons in the two generations above me who had known Mrs. Wharton well and who often confirmed these impressions. All of which is perfectly consistent with the picture, also drawn by Lubbock, of a woman who was a true friend among her intimates, congenial, humorous, loyal, and generous; an excellent mistress to her many servants and an indefatigable worker for charitable causes. Much of Wharton's formidable exterior in society and an abruptness amounting at times to rudeness may be explained by the terrible shyness which, as she wrote to a younger friend, Adele Burden, had shadowed her life:

Your letter went to my heart, and I am so glad you took the trouble to write it. How little we know each other, after all! I have always felt so utterly at my ease and comfortable with you. You have such a wonderful gift of making older people feel as if they were of your age that it never for a moment occurred to me that there was the least barrier of shyness between us. But as that dread disease martyrized me all through my youth, I feel great sympathy for all its victims.

I suspect that the reason Lubbock wrote so few books was that there were so few subjects available for his peculiar genius. A subject for his treatment had to be not only intimately known to him but bathed in nostalgia. Earlham Court and its garden, the masters of Eton, expatriates in Rome, the great Edith herself had to be re-created in illuminating prose that would enable the reader to share Lubbock's love, bedazzlement, and amusement. The method would always be pictorial—note the words "portrait," "pictures," and "shades" in his titles. He dealt with truth as it was outwardly presented or readily inferred; he made no pretense of opening closet doors or ferreting in desks. His art was like the art of Sargent: beauty was just as important as likeness; both were essential.

Yet his principal fictional protagonist, Channon, is covered over like Shakespeare's beautiful young friend by the image of the novel's title:

> But out alack, he was but one hour mine,
> The region cloud hath masked him from me now.

Courtship in Congreve

❧

Congreve through the generations has found himself constantly spanked for his morals, or lack thereof, from contemporary parsons who denounced him from the pulpit, to Thackeray, that king of Victorians masquerading as an eighteenth-century wit, who could not help wondering if the great dramatist, whose art seemed to justify a seat on the very peak of Parnassus, would not bring disapproving sniffs to the noses of the properer gods already there.

We can laugh at this in our own liberated day, but have you read him recently? He does go rather far. Making full allowance for the latitude of comedy, or even of farce, his heroes and villains still strut with astounding arrogance around a sleazy barnyard. Consider two of the former: Bellimour in *The Old Bachelor* and Mirabell in *The Way of the World*. Both are viewed as sympathetically by their creator as he seems capable of viewing men. They have charm and wit, and they are very much in love with equally charming and

First appeared in *New Criterion*, October 1986.

witty girls. Yet Bellimour, while wooing his Belinda, is quite as intently plotting the seduction of Mrs. Fondlewife, the spouse of an old fool whose name is proof, in a Congreve world, that the gods themselves will smile on his cuckolding. Mirabell is more constant to his enchanting Millament, yet he is represented, before the action of the play, as having deliberately hood-winked the villain Fainall into marrying his discarded mistress, whom he believes—erroneously, as it turns out—to be pregnant by himself. Here is how he justifies this conduct to his old love who, understandably enough, finds herself wretched in her new union:

> If the familiarities of our loves had produced that conse-quence of which you were apprehensive, where could you have fixed a father's name with credit, but on a hus-band? I knew Fainall to be a man lavish of his morals, an interested and professing friend, a false and design-ing lover; yet one whose wit and outward fair behaviour have gained a reputation with the town enough to make that woman stand excused who has suffered herself to be won by his addresses. A better man ought not to have been sacrificed to the occasion; a worse had not answered to the purpose.

What the standards of the barnyard seem to boil down to is that Fainall is fair game to be cheated because he is a creep, and that Mirabell is justified in cheating him because he has charm. And as for Bellimour, is a healthy young man to give up sex while he is obliged to go through the lengthy ritual of courtship? Of course not. Such virtue is expected only of the impotent.

Courtship and Congreve

I suggest that Congreve is not entirely joking when he tells us through the mouths of his female characters that men are inconstant creatures who will marry their inamoratas only if the latter stick it out. The game of courtship has perfectly definite rules. For the man it is to huff and to puff, to breathe deathless passion that neither he nor the woman addressed believes, and to do everything in his power to seduce her—as he is simultaneously seducing others. The woman's game is to hold him off with enticing mockery and yield not so much as a kiss until she has led him firmly to the altar. The penalties in the game are all for the woman; she who yields prematurely is labeled a "whore" by all, including her conqueror, nor can she ever thereafter hope to marry a gentleman unless she resorts to the subterfuge suggested by Mirabell. Yet the word "whore," at least as used in *The Old Bachelor* to describe the unfortunate Silvia, is without any sharp pejorative sense. She has been caught offside and been penalized, so to speak, a fatal number of yards. She has lost the game, to be sure; she is now a whore. But there are plenty of nice whores. One doesn't whip them at the cart tail. Silvia in the end is even allowed to marry a minor and ridiculous character.

What has probably most shocked people through the ages about Congreve is that he seems really to have accepted this concept as a valid social system. We have recently learned in a biography of Velásquez that even the greatest artist may care more for fashion than anything else in life. To Congreve it was bad to be a cuckold, no matter how little one cared for one's wife. Why? Society decreed it. And it was bad to lose one's maidenhead before marriage, although perfectly acceptable to commit adultery afterward. Why? Society ordained it. Today he would violate *our* fashion, because it is still fashionable to believe in enduring love after marriage, however rare it may be becoming.

Or *did* he believe in it? Is that the one note of sentiment that leaks through? He never, like Oscar Wilde, tries to reconcile his cynical characters in the last act to the wedded bliss of the late Victorian illusion. But he seems to allow us to speculate that Mirabell and Millament may have a happy life together. Or is his ghost laughing up his sleeve at me? Who knows? All that I can be sure of is that he had a passionate faith in the power of language. Only Shakespeare himself had a cadence in his prose like Congreve's. Mirabell can mock like Hamlet. Hear him tell how he tried to get the good will of Millament's absurd old aunt:

I did as much as man could, with any reasonable conscience; I proceeded to the very last act of flattery with her, and was guilty of a song in her commendation. Nay, I got a friend to put her into a lampoon, and compliment her with the imputation of an affair with a young fellow, which I carried so far, that I told her the malicious town took notice that she was grown fat of a sudden; and when she lay in of a dropsy, persuaded her she was reported to be in labour. The devil's in't, if an old woman is to be flattered further, unless a man should endeavour downright personally to debauch her: and that my virtue forbade me.

Clarissa Revisited

❧

*C**larissa* strikes me as a literary miracle. A novel in epistolary form of more than a million words about the attempted seduction and ultimate rape of a virtuous young woman by an almost maniacally obsessed rake, professedly written "to warn the inconsiderate and thoughtless of the one sex against the base arts and designs of specious contrivers of the other," would seem in an era of "sexual revolution" about as "irrelevant" as a literary endeavor could be. And if we turn to the prosy second volume of *Pamela* or attempt to wade through the turgid volumes of *Sir Charles Grandison*, Richardson's only other works of fiction, we find him just as tedious and sententious as his proclaimed homiletic purpose would lead us to expect.

It is not only the subject of the novel that might seem to repel the modern reader. Why should the two opponents in the long siege of chastity spend the major part of their days at their writing desk, recording not only the

First appeared in *Explorations*, Vol. IV, Lafayette, Louisiana, Special Series 1990.

few events and manifold personal reflections of the immediate past, but, in *ipsissimis verbis*, all the dialogues in which they have engaged? Why is it necessary for the author to repeat so endlessly the vengeful sentiments of the heroine's family, her own self-recriminations and lamentations, and the villain's gleeful, Iagoesque exultations? Why is every point made, literally, a hundred times? And why, for that matter, some exasperated reader might exclaim, does not the wronged Clarissa cease her chest-beating, take the earnest advice of all who truly care for her welfare, and marry her repentant ravisher? Pamela, after all, did so in the eponymous novel—though Pamela, of course, had not been raped. She had managed to hold on to her virtue and sell out in a bull market.

Yet the sure mark that we are faced with a work of unique power is that all abbreviated editions of *Clarissa* are dull. "Duller," I suppose I should say, in the view of those who persist in finding the unexpurgated text boring. There seems to be something in the tale of Clarissa Harlowe and Robert Lovelace that demands the full treatment which Richardson accords it. Oh, I don't say that one couldn't cut a bit in the long section where Clarissa is held a virtual prisoner in her family's house. She really doesn't need two relentlessly unforgiving uncles—one would be quite enough. And I think even the warmest Richardson fan would admit that the story sags after Clarissa's death and that the outpourings of grief and guilt could be curtailed. But these are minor matters. The great length of the work is essentially necessary.

Necessary for what? For a hypnotic effect? Well, that may indeed be in it. The novel can obtain an uncanny hold on the reader who will surrender himself to it. As Dr. Johnson famously observed, one does not read *Clarissa* for the plot, but for the sentiment. And for that sentiment one need not share Clarissa's high assessment of virginity any more than one need share Antigone's stress on the holy duty of burial (as pointed out by T. C. Duncan Eaves and Ben D. Kimpel in their great life of Richardson) or Hester Prynne's sense of sin for an adultery that in our day (given the circumstances of her forced marriage and the long absence and probable death of her husband) would be deemed without stain. No, the sentiment for which we read the book lies in Clarissa's burning passion for virtue and Lovelace's equally burning one to destroy it.

Let me outline the bare bones of the plot for which we do *not* read *Clarissa*. The heroine, beautiful, intellectual, refined, pious, generous, infinitely loyal, a paragon of upper-middle-class virtue, and dowered, to boot, with wealth and the finest, most discriminating taste, is courted in marriage by the handsome and dashing rake Lovelace, of superior birth but vastly inferior morals.

Because Lovelace has seized upon the perfunctory refusal of the originally courted older sister to turn his attention to her lovelier junior, the venomous and jealous Arabella, aided by brother James, who fears Clarissa's greater favor in the eyes of their rich bachelor uncles and resents the already shown preference of her in their late grandfather's will, easily produces enough damaging evidence of Lovelace's rakish past (including a duel with James in which Lovelace has contemptuously spared the former's life) to induce the Harlowes to break off the match. They go further and command

Clarissa to marry a repulsive old miser, Soames, whose vast acreage conveniently abuts the Harlowe estates. When Clarissa refuses, she is imprisoned in the house, and, fearing that she may be actually forced to marry Soames, a fear falsely inflamed by Lovelace with whom she is in secret correspondence and to whom she is, despite his bad reputation with women, reluctantly attracted, she flees with him, assured of his honorable matrimonial intentions.

But once in his clutches she finds herself in a much viler prison. He houses her in what she soon enough discovers to be a house of ill fame, all of whose inhabitants are in his pay, and finds plenty of reasons to delay the nuptial ceremony. The rest of the tale abounds with the elaborate stratagems he devises to gain access to her bed without placing a ring on her finger. When all else fails, he drugs and rapes her. After this he genuinely offers marriage, but, needless to say, a woman of her fine character now won't have him, preferring to succumb to a fatal illness brought on by her Lucretian determination not to survive the loss of her honor. She forgives the now-wretched Lovelace on her deathbed, but he is soon after killed in a duel with an avenging cousin of his victim.

This simple morality tale has been woven into a literary tapestry that evokes an emotional reaction in the reader somewhere between the lofty response to the majestic sweep of Milton's verse in *Paradise Lost* and the indignation aroused by the "bad guys" in a soap opera. I have to mention the latter because I do not know of any other fictional classic that quickens the pulse of anger as does the section of *Clarissa* that deals with the cruelty of the Harlowes to the heroine. They are worse than Lovelace himself for they lack the excuse of his passion or the mitigation of his own cheerful acceptance of the evil in his soul. How does Richardson accomplish his remarkable effect, and why does he utterly fail to do so in his other two novels?

The answer must lie in the intense drama of the contrast between the characters of Clarissa and Lovelace, a contrast kept always before the reader's eyes as they are always locked in battle. Their conflict takes the book right out of the author's hands and reduces to trivia his alleged purpose of warning thoughtless young women of the dangers of seduction and parents of the risks inherent in the arbitrary selection of their mates. Richardson's vivid imagination and deeply feeling heart have been caught up in his story. There are other examples in fiction of just the right character in just the right situation fitting so well with an author's peculiar talent as to produce a novel that stands head and shoulders above his other works. Becky Sharp and her determination to climb above her birth and fortune did that to *Vanity Fair*, as Sir Willoughby Patterne and his need to hang on to his fiancée did it to *The Egoist*.

It might seem that Clarissa is a more important character than Lovelace because the novel loses much of its interest with her death. But her death ends the battle that is the real theme of the book. She is still more important, however, in that she is the focus of all the other characters. It is her very perfection that arouses their envy and hate. Her light shines too brightly before them, and they strike blindly to put it out. That is the terrifying thing about the novel. No one in the book can quite endure the contrast she offers. Richardson's picture of the wolf pack and the stricken doe is a grim one, even in the century of the Holocaust, because it admits of no exceptions other than the heroine herself, who inevitably takes on a Christ-like aspect.

Let me itemize their hostilities. Clarissa's parents, siblings, uncles, and aunt are obvious enough. They are unanimous in banishing her from their hearts for her rejection of Soames. But their motives differ. Arabella is jealous of Lovelace, and her brother James wants to discredit Clarissa with the uncles for mercenary reasons. The older generation resent her independence. Their real wish is not so much to marry her to Soames as to dominate her, to *own* her. Her virtue is much less threatening if it is *their* property. Indeed, may it not then become *their* virtue? One of her mother's bitterest complaints is that the neighbors despise the Harlowes for their treatment of Clarissa. The family has actually lost virtue in losing her as the gods in Valhalla lose their youth when Freia is torn from their midst by the giants.

And this extends, if to a much lesser extent, to the characters who are well-disposed to Clarissa: her old nurse, Judith Norton, Mrs. Howe, Colonel Morden, and even her adoring friend and faithful correspondent, Miss Howe. For none of them change their opinion that Clarissa should marry Lovelace, even when they discover the full horror of her rape and the circumstances leading up to it. None of them can exist on Clarissa's exalted moral level; all urge compromise. They cannot accept the simple impossibility that Clarissa should swear to love and obey a man who has done what he has done. She is indeed too good for their world.

Miss Howe is the character who comes closest to seeing that there may be a satanic element in what is happening to her friend. She writes to Clarissa that her perfection may have tempted the devil to try her:

> It must be some man, or some worse spirit in the shape of one, that, formed on purpose, was to be sent to invade you; while as many other such spirits, as there are persons in your family, were permitted to take possession, severally, in one dark hour, of the heart of everyone of it.

And Lovelace, writing to his close but disapproving friend Belfort, seems to agree with her: "Miss Howe will tell thee: she says I am the *devil*. By my conscience I think he has at present a great part of me."

The great danger in the novel is that Clarissa, being almost virtue epitomized, will become a bore. She is splendidly saved from this fate by being endowed with some very human traits. She is prim, compulsively neat, sharp of tongue, quick to criticize, and almost self-indulgent in her fixed determination to justify the cruelty of her relatives by overemphasizing her own tiniest fault. Yet her deep kindness to inferiors and her splendid courage in adversity make her intensely sympathetic. And when Richardson shows how she manages, locked up in a brothel and supervised by a ghoulish madam, to look her best, even stylish, in the few dresses she has managed to bring with her, this hint of harmless vanity turns her into a not only pitiable but an actually lovable character.

As Lovelace continues a persecution that makes him as loathed by the reader as his victim is loved, Clarissa is reduced at last to a state where she has no comfort but in her God and in her pen. To us the pen seems the greater comfort of the two. It is as if the words of her letters, the words of her novel, the language that is what distinguishes men from beasts, might be almost enough to transcend all the multitudinous villainies of the world.

She has been aware of this strength even before her escape from her family's house. "At the worst I have got a pencil of black, and another of red lead which I use in my drawings, and my patterns shall serve as paper if I have no other."

And as Lovelace's prisoner she must continue to write, even if she has no one to correspond with. She informs Miss Howe: "And indeed, my dear, I know not how to forbear writing. I have now no other employment or diversion. And I must write on, altho' I were not to send it to anybody."

Clarissa, from the beginning to the end of her story, seems to me without a moral flaw. Yet Richardson purports to endow her with one small but fatal fault. She has disobeyed her parents in running off with a man with whom she had no business to be in secret communication. It is by that forbidden correspondence that he has been able to play on her fears that she may be actually forced into a marriage with Soames. Had she not listened to him, but stayed and simply refused to accept Soames as a husband, according to Richardson, her family would in the end have accepted her decision. But how could Clarissa be sure of that? She has been given reason to apprehend incarceration in the lonely moated castle of an uncle, the calling of a bribed priest, possibly even the use of drugs. And she has had no reason to suspect the depths of degradation of Lovelace's character.

All she knows is that he has the reputation of a rake, as had, before their marriages, many respectable husbands of her acquaintance. No, I maintain, despite the argument of her creator, that Clarissa's moral character is just about perfect.

Lovelace, on the other hand, progresses from a sympathetic and attractive character to the fiend whom we are delighted to see run through by Colonel Morden's rapier. At first we see his compulsion to overcome women's virtue as a kind of lively sport. He scorns the seduction of nonvirgins, the "leavings" of other men, except for an occasional married woman. He avows his preference for the unstained daughters of good family, although the presence in his private brothel of two lowborn ex-mistresses makes one doubt that he has always been consistent in this respect. The process of seduction is the main point of his game; compared to it, the "crowning act" is merely "a vapour, a bubble." The first kiss that he implants on Clarissa's chaste lips delights him more than "the ultimatum with any other woman." And he claims always scrupulously to observe the rules he has set himself:

> To shun common women. To marry off a former mistress before he took a new one. To set the mother above want if her friends were cruel: to maintain a lady handsomely in her lying-in. To provide for the little one according to the mother's degree. And to go mourning for her if she died in childbed.

What he really wants is domination, the assertion of his total will over his victim. He exults in fantasies of himself as a kind of sultan, extending his vision of conquest over Anne Howe as well as Clarissa herself:

> How sweetly pretty to see the two lovely friends, when humbled and tame, both sitting in the darkest corner of a room, arm in arm, weeping and sobbing for each other. And I their emperor, their then acknowledged emperor, reclined on a sophee, in the same room, Grand Signor like, uncertain to which I should first throw over my handkerchief.

In similar lordly oriental fashion he includes in his fantasy bastard twin sons by the subdued Clarissa:

> Let me perish, Belfort, if I would not forgo the brightest diadem in the world, for the pleasure of seeing twin Lovelaces at each charming breast, drawing forth its first sustenance. . . . I now, methinks, behold this most charming of women in this sweet office, pressing with her fine fingers the generous flood into the purple mouths of each eager hunter by turns.

And he sees Clarissa's eyes "full of wishes for the sake of the pretty varlets . . . that I would condescend to put on nuptial fetters."

This picture of the reduced and acquiescent Clarissa is of the sort that betrays private sexual fantasies in an author. I can hardly resist winking at the round complacent countenance of the great moralist in the Mason Chamberlain portrait and murmuring, "Really, Mr. Richardson!"

Lovelace's initial plan, when the seduction has been

completed, is not to marry Clarissa—she will then be unworthy to be his bride—but to cohabit with her. This will not only establish his total possession and give him a charming mistress to whom he will have no need to be faithful; it will gratifyingly humiliate the proud but upstart Harlowes who have dared to revile him. When Clarissa, however, proves unseduceable, eluding him at every turn, and when her original predisposition in his favor turns to hate, he resolves to use force. He still hopes that rape will subdue his victim to the point of accepting cohabitation, but if it fails of this effect, he is now at last willing to consider matrimony. He will not, he supposes, be in honor obliged to consider a stain in his bride that he has forced upon her, provided she does not publicize her disgrace.

Of course, the ravished Clarissa refuses even to consider marriage, and Lovelace goes almost mad with frustration and with what begins to have something of the appearance of genuine repentance. But he can never really understand why his offer of marriage does not make up for all his deception, his kidnapping, and his rape. He has murdered Clarissa; that is the long and short of it, and Morden's slaying of him in a duel is virtually an execution. Oscar Wilde's Danny Deaver claims that each man kills the thing he loves, but is it really love? Richardson would have scornfully denied such Freudian sophistry.

Tennessee Williams

The Last Puritan

Under our peculiar American brand of Calvinism sex was a thing to be boxed up in marriage, or, at the very least, confined to persons of opposite sex and similar age and caste. And even today, with variance generally permitted, there lurks a tendency to perpetuate a system of boxes. If we have created a box for homosexuals, there is still a feeling, shared by many gays, that they should stay in it. Yet sex is an energy that pervades all of our imagination and most of our acts and that manifests itself in every human relationship. It took the genius of Tennessee Williams to dramatize this universality. His heroes and heroines are sexual impulses, his plots a kind of sexual intercourse. The presence of lust or love in every episode and piece of dialogue in his plays is what gives the warmth and glow even to his brutes and villains. Violence in Williams is usually manifested by a rape or a castration.

First appeared in somewhat different form in *Dictionary of Literary Biography*, Documentary Series, Vol. IV, Gale Research Co., Detroit, 1984.

His is a world where the young and beautiful male is god. Whatever coarseness, meanness, or even cruelty is to be found in such figures as Stanley Kowalski, Brick Pollitt, or Chance Wayne, they dominate their plays with a swagger that recalls the strutting roosters that spell such certain ruin for the hypnotized hens of Restoration comedy. Elia Kazan, a poet among directors, invested the production of *A Streetcar Named Desire* with a contrast of light and shade that held the brutal Stanley and his victim Blanche in a limbo between reality and fantasy suitable to the mood of the drama. In his notes for the play Kazan described Stanley as a "walking phallus."

But there is a marked difference between the stage world of Williams and that of Congreve and Wycherley. For there is something enigmatic, even androgynous in the Williams hero. One critic commented on Marlon Brando's "mincing interpretation" of the role of Stanley. Brick's broken ankle in *Cat on a Hot Tin Roof* is suggestive of castration, the grim fate that in fact awaits Chance after the closing curtain of *Sweet Bird of Youth*. And the atmosphere in which these characters move and breathe is sufficiently erogenous to invest their every act with a sexual connotation. Even the most horrible things that happen to Williams's people are suggestive of masochistic pleasure.

Williams's published correspondence with Donald Windham, roughly covering the span of World War II, from any participation in which heart trouble exempted him, shows the playwright actively at work, seeking all over the country the success that was to elude him until 1945. Yet the reader of these letters would never guess that a war was going on except for an occasional reference to the greater availability on the streets, for sexual encounters, of sailors and GIs. But Williams, a John the Baptist of the coming sexual revolution, might claim that, far from having been alienated or exotic, he was closer to the pulse of the America emerging from Armageddon than any who had donned a uniform.

He has never made any secret of his homosexuality. In his candid memoirs he describes how early he accepted it, with all its implications. But that does not mean that his psyche was not ridden with guilt feelings. It is almost impossible, given the southern Calvinist culture in which he grew up, that this should not have been so. In several of his plays homosexuals receive hideous punishments. His art may owe to the cultivation of forbidden fruit some of the intense appeal of its peculiar blend of love and cruelty. This is also true of Proust, a distasteful reminder of how much writers may owe to the tabus and repressions of unemancipated societies. The New England guilty conscience produced *The Scarlet Letter* as well as many blighted lives.

Williams's was peculiarly the genius of his era. America in 1945 had won a war that seemed to have made the world safe for nuclear destruction. The old gods, all of them, were hustled offstage by the impatient young. Sex took their place, and Williams was its prophet. But his reign was not eternal. By the early 1960s he was beginning to lose both his critical and popular following. He seemed to be repeating himself, to be blurring the sharpness of his focus. In 1969 he suffered a severe nervous collapse, aggravated by drugs and alcohol. Despite a valiant comeback, he never quite recaptured his old stature. Why?

It may have been simply the lack in his theatre of what the philosopher Morris Cohen used to call "thought content." As tolerance in sexual matters lightened people's hearts, audiences began to tire of the fiery drama of repressed guilt and masochism and to look for more than anguish in the drama of love. Williams had less to say to them now. Consider the story in *Cat on a Hot Tin Roof*. A fine, tense first act shows Brick and Maggie fighting in their bedroom in Big Daddy's house over what appears to be the hopeless wreck of their marriage. Brick, who has a broken leg, hobbles back and forth between his bed and the bar table, drinking incessantly and lashing his frantic, adoring spouse with the icy retorts of his indifference and contempt. We do not know what is wrong with Brick, nor do we, in this act, need to know. The crackling dialogue is enough.

Unfortunately, the rest of the play fails to explain Brick. Like Hamlet in T. S. Eliot's famous essay, his emotion is inexpressible because it is in excess of the facts as they are given to us. He may be suffering from guilt over repressed homosexuality, or from guilt at his possible partial responsibility for the suicide of his best friend, who was definitely suffering from guilt over repressed homosexuality, but in either event it is not enough to have caused quite such devastating anguish, or, if it is, it could not be cured by the slick improvised happy ending tacked on by Williams at the suggestion of the hit-seeking Elia Kazan.

Ultimately, Williams, like Oscar Wilde, shunned these questions to wrap himself in the toga of art. What were the couplings of ordinary folk but grist for the mill of the great writer? The aging movie actress in *Sweet*

Bird of Youth, taking leave of her gigolo the morning after, might be an aging male homosexual sneering at the poor punk whom he has bought for the night:

"Of course, you were crowned with laurel in the beginning; your gold hair was wreathed with laurel, but the gold is thinning, and the laurel has withered. Face it— pitiful monster. Of course, I know I'm one too. But one with a difference. Do you know what that difference is? No, you don't know. We are two monsters, but with this difference between us. Out of the passion and torment of my existence I have created a thing that I can unveil, a sculpture almost heroic, that I can unveil, which is true. But you?"

The punk might have retorted, like Nietzsche, that dionysianism, undiluted, is, in the last analysis, only chaos. But it was a beautiful chaos in Williams's first plays, and it has won its creator a lasting niche in the story of American drama.

The Lyttelton–
Hart-Davis Letters

❧

When George Lyttelton, a retired housemaster of Eton, where he had been for many years a beloved and inspiring teacher of English, met his former student, the author and editor Rupert Hart-Davis, at the London dinner party in 1955 that was to spark their seven-year correspondence, Lyttelton was seventy-two and Hart-Davis forty-eight. The former complained that he was lonely and bored living in Suffolk, because there was nobody for him to talk to and nobody wrote to him. His old pupil, "flushed with wine," made a rash promise.

"I'll write to you, George."

"When will you start?"

"Next weekend."

"Right. I'll answer in the middle of the week."

The correspondence thus initiated continued unbroken until Lyttelton's death in 1962. It fills six short and delightful volumes that have been printed and reprinted in Great Britain and America and have evoked hundreds of appreciative letters to the editor from all over the world.

A part of the charm of these letters is their regularity and their close interconnection. Each epistler is careful to comment on the other's last; every question is scrupulously answered. The letters cover the events, large and small, of the writer's week: what he has read and thought about; gossip, both local and international; and the course (largely downward) of the great world around them. The comments are witty, at times bawdy, often profound, and, particularly in the case of Lyttelton, expressed in beautiful, pungent prose.

But perhaps what gives to the correspondence its peculiar liveliness is the contrast between the lives of the two writers. As Lyttelton puts it:

You know, Rupert, the fundamental—and slightly depressing—difference between my letters and yours is that yours are full of interesting things that you have done, and ditto people you have seen. I, having done neither, am reduced, largely, to not very inspiring chatter about what I have been reading—with an occasional diversion on to, say, gorillas and other large animals for which you do not share my taste. What can be done about it? Nothing that I myself can see. Shall I tell you what Miss Smith (nicknamed "the drip") said about teaching Eng. Lit. to girls who confuse Ben Jonson with Doctor Johnson and are not in the least abashed by her horror?

Of course, in many ways Lyttelton was in the better position; he had the time and leisure to polish his thoughts. He was a kind of Montaigne to whom the younger man, out in the great world, could bring chunks of source material for him to comment on. And he could make even the pettiest local news amusing.

Charlie Balls has, alas, left the village. No coarse laughter from you, please. It is a very common name in Suffolk, so much, say, that at a political meeting a loud shout of "Balls" is usually not a comment on what is being said on the platform, but merely one of the clan hailing another across the hall.

Lyttelton liked to play the role of the old curmudgeon, passed over, on the shelf, the hypercritical survivor of a golden age in a tacky present, and it is true that, compared to Hart-Davis, he was something of that, but a good deal less than he let on. He was still the "Honorable George," younger son of a viscount and related to half the old peerage, adored by Eton graduates and by his charming wife, five children (including the bandleader Humphrey Lyttelton), and many grandchildren, and sought out as a speaker at banquets and graduations. He even still worked as a part-time examiner for schools, and a recurring theme in his letters is the wonderful boners he has to correct in Shakespeare papers, such as the paraphrasing of the duke of Gaunt's "this dear, dear land" to "this very expensive land."

Yet it is certainly true that Lyttelton had his prejudices. He had little use for abstract art, too explicitly sexual novels, or obscure poetry. He didn't care for Joyce or D. H. Lawrence, and, as might be expected, F. R. Leavis was his particular bête noire. He clearly felt that England's greatest days were over; one shudders to think what he would have thought of the goings-on of the Royal Family in 1993. But there is a kind of splendor in his deep reverence for what he considered the departed glory of English prose, as written by Macaulay, Carlyle, and Dr. Johnson. Particularly the last.

> Do you ever get things quite wrong? Because here is the perfect defense: "What is obvious is not always known, what is known is not always present. Sudden fits of inadvertency will surprise vigilance; slight avocations will seduce attention, and casual eclipses of the mind will darken learning." Isn't it perfect? Johnson, of course.

Hart-Davis, on the other hand, lived aboundingly and much more enthusiastically in the very present present, publishing a book a week, traveling to Europe and America to meet authors and publishers, constantly entertaining and being entertained by the luminaries of the literary, political, and social worlds. And he managed at the same time to snatch hours from a crowded calendar to edit with a thousand footnotes his great edition of the letters of Oscar Wilde, which Richard Ellmann, definitive biographer of the latter, called a "landmark in modern scholarship."

But Hart-Davis had a very private life, in addition to his very public one, which he ultimately confessed to his correspondent. His second marriage (his first was to the actress Peggy Ashcroft) to Comfort, the mother of his three children, had become one in name only.

> Comfort is one of the (I suspect) many women whose sex instincts are in fact wholly directed to the production of

children, and when their quiver is full, they want no more (as they say in the courts) intercourse. So it was with her; when we married in 1933 she was passionate and gay, but after Adam's conception in 1942 she had had enough. I bore this enforced chastity for four years: if I had been a person who could flit from flower to flower, that might have provided a solution: but I am not: sex to me is indissolubly linked with love. And then in 1946 I met Ruth, and we fell in love like steel filings rushing to a magnet. It was touch and go whether we didn't elope immediately, but somehow we held on, for our families' sake. I told Comfort about it, and she took it wonderfully, saying she was rather relieved on the sexual side, but hoped I wouldn't break up the family. I said I wouldn't.

A design for living was worked out in which Hart-Davis and Ruth (who also worked in his office) shared a flat in London and a weekend cottage in Yorkshire, while he spent certain weeknights with Comfort at Bromsden Farm outside London. Once when he was ill, the two women took turns nursing him!

Hart-Davis had some trepidation in telling Lyttelton of this; it was only in the third year of the correspondence that he did so. He had been afraid that his old friend might be shocked. And perhaps a couple of decades earlier he might have been. But now he heartily approved. Besides, the writing and reading of these letters has become a vital part of the older man's life; nothing could be allowed to alter the warm and friendly tone in which they were couched. It was Lyttelton's last chance to make a contribution, however tiny, in

words, wonderful words, to the noble body of English
literature that had been the mainstay of his existence. If
to Hart-Davis the correspondence constituted the diary
of a life, to Lyttelton it had become life itself.

When he misplaced one of Hart-Davis's letters, and
the latter joshed him about it, he replied, in all seriousness: "Nasty little sarcasm about my losing your letter—
like chaffing a man about the loss of a dear friend. I am
still full of chagrin whenever I think of it. It shall never
happen again."

The friends were highly selective in the funny stories
which they relayed to each other. Here is one of
Lyttelton's:

A man in a railway carriage, after studying the *Financial
Times*, threw it on the floor, exclaiming: "The Stock-
Exchange be buggered!" and then saw to his horror that
he was not, as he thought, alone, but that there was an
elderly lady in the far corner. He apologized profusely,
but all she said was, "I am afraid your wish cannot be
granted, as I read this morning that the bottom had fall-
en out of the market."

And from Hart-Davis:

A couple, twenty years married, had a fearful row.
The wife told the husband exactly what she thought of
him, ending: "And on top of all that, we've had your old
mother living with us for ten years."

Husband: "*My* mother? I always thought she was *your*
mother!"

End of story.

Perhaps I can give some sense of the flavor of the correspondence with a few samples of the way each incident related by one writer triggers off an old memory, quotation, or anecdote in the mind of the other. Hart-Davis's speaking of a "tutor" reminds Lyttelton of a dear old Victorian snob great-aunt, who, when a relative married a headmaster of great distinction, remarked gloomily, "I do think it is rather (pronounced as in 'gather') dowdy to marry a tootor." A reference to the poet Walter de la Mare leads to the recollection that it was he who had pointed out what splendid names for a heroine and villain Lady Angina Pectoris and Sir Rheumatoid Arthritis would be. And, speaking of medicine, Lyttelton's doctor was not impressed by court physicians; he quotes him as saying: "Oh, yes, those Windsor surgeons; he was probably knighted for cutting King Edward's corns."

Hart-Davis writes that Lady Diana Cooper avoids parking tickets by sticking a note under her windshield wiper: "Have mercy. Am taking sad child to cinema." He describes an expensive and fence-straddling opinion of learned counsel as an exact parallel to the old problem and its answer about the sex of a canary: "Give the bird a lump of sugar; if it is a he, he will eat it, and if it is a she, she will." And Lyttelton recalls affectionately an old lawyer uncle's terse bill sent to a cousin: "To conversation on telephone about Captain X's pension and agreeing it would be small: £1.6.8." Hart-Davis starts one letter: "Your unedifying visit to the pub reminds me of the Chinese proverb: 'The dragon in shallow waters becomes the butt of shrimp.'"

When Lyttelton leaves his sponge in a hotel he

writes: "I think of putting up a notice like that one at the Athenaeum: 'Will the clergyman who stole my umbrella kindly return it. The club consists half of gentlemen and half of clergymen, and it is clear that no gentleman would steal an umbrella.'"

Lyttelton wrote his weekly letter right up to the end, when he was stricken with cancer of the liver. The last was a brief note, dictated to his wife, five days before his death:

There is nothing in anything except my gratitude and the wonderfulness of Pamela (she mustn't cross that out). So what then? I am not even a chaos—I am a vast infinity. She will write you any more, if there is anything. Love to Ruth and bless you both. Oh, the boredom!

Henry James

The Theatre Years

Henry James's "theatre years," as the period of his life from 1890 to 1894 (*aetat* forty-seven to fifty-two) is usually designated, began with the moderately successful production of the play he dramatized from his novel *The American*, and ended with the hisses and catcalls that disgraced the first-night audience of *Guy Domville*. He had dramatized *Daisy Miller* as early as 1881, and *The Outcry* as late as 1909, but these theatre years were the only ones in which he dedicated his principal energies to the stage. It was all in the vain hope of increasing his income. His fiction had enjoyed consistent praise from the more enlightened critics, but his sales had never even approched those of such lesser literary lights as William Dean Howells, F. Marion Crawford, or Mrs. Humphrey Ward.

After the dismal debut of *Guy Domville* James wisely renounced the theatre, at least as his major occupation, and returned to his true medium with this touching and gallant entry in a notebook: "I take up my old pen again—the pen of all my old unforgettable efforts and sacred struggles. To myself—today I need say no more. Large and full and high the future still opens. It is now indeed that I may do the work of my life. And I will."

But he felt a very human reluctance to face up to the fact that his theatrical efforts had been of no profit, not merely to his purse, but to his art. Surely there must have been *some* gain to him as a writer after all that toil and sweat! He continued: "Has a *part* of all this wasted passion and squandered time been simply the precious lesson, taught me in that roundabout and devious, that cruelly expensive, way, *of the singular value for a narrative plan too* of the (I don't know *what* adequately to call it) divine principle of the scenario?"

Leon Edel, foremost of Jacobite biographers and critics, agrees with James: "The theatre had taught him rigid economy and how to allow a situation to unfold without the intervention of the narrator; how to obtain intensity from a given situation by extracting all the elements of drama it contained."

What Edel is saying is that James, after the theatre years, tightened his plots, reducing his action to what was essential to the basic theme of the novel, eliminating as far as possible the "omniscient author" and restricting the reader's vision to what was seen and felt, in *The Golden Bowl* and *The Wings of the Dove*, by half a dozen characters, or, better yet, in *The Ambassadors*, by only one. But I submit that this "tidying up" of the novel form, to make it as different as possible from what James deemed the "fluid puddings" of Tolstoy and Dostoyevsky, had been a life process, starting well before his theatrical experiments and not in the least affected by them. His plays were not only much less dramatic but less well organized than the novels that preceded them, let alone those that followed.

James's total misconception of what it took to make a good play was the more extraordinary in that he was a lifelong avid theatregoer and even claimed to have the French drama "in his pocket." He believed that a theatre audience had lower taste than the reading public and might appreciate his covering the boards with imperious ladies of middle age who order everyone about, mock villains who candidly admit their villainy, servants who comment on the inanity of their masters, and high-spirited young lovers who dart about uttering vapid repartée in clipped phrases. None of this would he have ever even considered putting in a novel. He should have known that the theatre never forgives those who condescend to it.

What he *did* learn from these years was the multitude of things he could do in a novel that he *couldn't* do on the stage, and all by the magic of his incomparable prose, of his vividly illustrative, finely evocative, richly meshed descriptions of persons and places, and by taking his reader into the minds and imaginations of characters as sensitive as himself. What is Lambert Strether in *The Ambassadors*, and the beautiful vision of Paris that filters through his mind to the destruction of all his old values, but a perfect example of just what the playwright is unable to do?

James wrote of the great assistance that the discipline of writing scenarios was to prove when he returned to fiction, and he was always thereafter to draft one before starting a novel. But a reading of the ninety-page "scenario" he produced for *The Ambassadors* shows it to be merely a detailed outline of the plot. That this kind of preparation was a valuable aid in the composition of well-crafted novels seems undeniable, but did he have to write half a dozen plays to discover it?

Moving on to the question of speech, which is largely what any play consists of, it is interesting to note that many examples of dialogue in the great novels of the middle period that immediately preceded the theatre years, i.e., *The American, The Portrait of a Lady, The Tragic Muse*, and *The Bostonians*, are far more tensely dramatic than any to be found in the plays. Let me contrast two "scenes," the first from *The Portrait of a Lady* and the second from James's comedy, *Disengaged*.

In the first, Isabel, subject of the "portrait," has finally realized, not only that the "sterile dilettante" she has married, Gilbert Osmond, was after her fortune, but that he actually now hates her for not turning out to be the kind of clay he could model into a puppet. Their outward relations have so far been coolly civilized, but a crisis arises when she learns in Rome that her beloved cousin Ralph is dying in England. She goes to her husband's study to tell him she must go to Ralph's bedside. I have stripped the passage of all the descriptive prose that makes it one of James's finest and left only the actual dialogue between the couple. Isabel speaks first.

—Excuse me for disturbing you.

—When I come to your room, I always knock.

—I forgot. I had something else to think of. My cousin's dying.

—Ah, I don't believe that. He was dying when we married; he'll outlive us all.

—My aunt has telegraphed me. I must go to Gardencourt.

—Why must you go to Gardencourt?

—To see Ralph before he dies.

—I don't see the need of it. He came to see you here. I didn't like that. I thought his being in Rome a great mistake. But I tolerated it because it was to be the last time you should see him. Now you tell me it's not to have been the last. Ah, you're not grateful!

—What am I to be grateful for?

—For my not having interfered when he was here.

—Oh, yes, I am. I remember perfectly how distinctly you let me know you didn't like it. I was very glad when he went away.

—Let him alone then. Don't run after him.

—I must go to England.

—I shall not like it if you do.

—Why should I mind that? You won't like it if I don't. You like nothing I do or don't do. You pretend to think I lie.

—That's why you must go then? Not to see your cousin, but to take revenge on me.

—I know nothing about revenge.

—I do. Don't give me an occasion.

—You're only too eager to take one. You wish immensely that I would commit some folly.

—I should be grateful in that case if you disobeyed me.

—If I disobeyed you?

—Let it be clear. If you leave Rome today, it will be a piece of the most deliberate, the most calculated opposition.

—How can you call it calculated? I received my aunt's telegram but three minutes ago.

—You calculate rapidly; it's a great accomplishment. I don't see why we should prolong our discussion; you know my wish.

—You've no reason for such a wish, and I've every reason for going. I can't tell you how unjust you seem to me. But I think you know. It's your own opposition that's calculated. It's malignant.

In James's *Disengaged*, the members of a stylish English house party, all immersed in more or less insincere extramarital flirtations, plan a cruel practical joke, for totally unconvincing motives, on a naïve but upright army captain to persuade him that his innocent politeness to a dunce of a girl has compromised her to the point where honor requires him to propose marriage. When the unfortunate young man does so, and is speedily accepted, the group relents and decides to rescue him by palming off their least deserving member on the girl. James now belatedly attempts to turn Captain Prime into his hero, but it is too late—we are convinced of his hopeless stupidity. The play degenerates into a mishmash of sudden exits and entrances as the characters flit on and off the stage scattering ambiguous persiflage. Was *this*, one wonders, what James meant by the tight organization he had learned from his new trade? Here is the scene where the heroine, Mrs. Jasper, who has found to her surprise that she likes Captain Prime, who has fallen in love with her, urges the distracted man to hold to his absurd engagement until she can devise some socially acceptable excuse to get him out of it.

Prime: I can't keep it up, you know, Mrs. Jasper; I really can't.

Mrs. Jasper: You must, a few days—to gain time.

Prime: To lose it, you mean. Why go so far?

Mrs. Jasper: Why indeed did you? You've gone too far!

Prime: That's just what I feel!

Mrs. Jasper: Too far to retreat, I mean. Therefore you must advance!

Prime: To my destruction?

Mrs. Jasper: We'll avert your destruction! Trust to your star; something will turn up!

Prime: That's the difficulty—that *you're* my star! Something *has* turned up.

Mrs. Jasper (ardently): It has—it has; it will turn up again!

Prime: The more it turns up the less I can advance. How can I be "engaged" when I love another woman?

Mrs. Jasper (startled): *Do* you love another woman?

Prime: Mrs. Jasper, I love *you*!

Mrs. Jasper (with alarm): Don't utter it! Go—fly!

Prime: Mrs. Jasper, I adore you!

Mrs. Jasper: You *can't*—not *yet*!

Prime: When *can* I then? Tell me when!

Mrs. Jasper: I must look about me—I must see!

Prime: You'll tell me tomorrow?

Mrs. Jasper: Tomorrow.

Prime: You won't put me off?

Mrs. Jasper (at the end of her patience): Not if you'll go.

Prime: Do you like me?

Mrs. Jasper (to get him off): I like you!

Prime: Would you marry me?

Mrs. Jasper: I'll tell you tomorrow!
Prime: Early?
Mrs. Jasper: About this time!
Prime (at the door): Noon? Angel! *(Exits)*
Mrs. Jasper (laughing): Lamb!

Could that be the same author who had written the tense interchanges between Isabel and Osmond, or between Mme. de Bellegarde and Newman in *The American*, or between Olive Chancellor and Basil Ransom, or Olive and Mrs. Burrage, in *The Bostonians*, or between Hyacinth Robinson and Paul Muniment in *The Princess Casamassima*, or between Miriam Rooth and Peter Sherringham in *The Tragic Muse*? One might almost argue that the business of playwriting, far from helping him as a novelist, had actually cost James some of the finely intense sense of drama that he had developed in writing the fiction of his middle period.

An example of this might be found in his dramatization of *The American*. The passages in the novel that relate the interviews between the unreconstructed and remorseless feudal aristocrat, Mme. de Bellegarde, and the rough-and-ready hero from across the seas who dares to aspire to her daughter's hand, could be put into a play without any change. For example:

"Your daughter's very beautiful," he said at last.
"She's very perverse," the old woman returned.
"I'm glad to hear it," he smiled. "It makes me hope."
"Hope what?"
"That she'll consent some day to marry me."
She slowly got up. "That really is your great idea?"

"Yes. Will you give it any countenance?"

Madame de Bellegarde looked at him hard and shook her head. "No!"

"Will you then just let me alone with my chance?"

"You don't know what you ask. I'm a very proud and meddlesome old person."

"Well, I'm very rich," he returned with a world of desperate intention.

She fixed her eyes on the floor, and he thought it probable she was weighing the reasons in favor of resenting his so calculated directness. But at last looking up, "How rich?" she simply articulated.

But in the play James eliminated the whole exciting story of Newman's contested courtship of Claire de Cintré, skipping straight to the announced engagement after a first act in which Newman has crudely informed her brother that he is seeking as a mate "a first class woman, the product of a long civilization and a great cultivation." Imagine a hero saying *that* on the stage! And when we first see Mme. de Bellegarde she is already seeking to get out of her commitment by pretending to believe that Newman is keeping a mistress openly in his house. She is petty and mean, whereas in the novel she is proudly and splendidly evil.

When James sought to emulate Dumas *fils* in his play *Tenants*, on his rash boast that he had the French theatre in his pocket, he stripped a characteristic Dumas situation of all its inherent drama. The power of Dumas's *Le Fils Naturel* lies in its vivid depiction of the passionate resentment of an abandoned bastard son who grows up to gain the world and scorn the belatedly offered recognition of the father who now sees him as a social asset. In James's handling of a similar situation, the son, comfortably raised by an affluent widowed mother, is quite unaware that he is not the issue of her late husband until, to foil a blackmailer, she enlightens him. She then marries the true father, and all live happily thereafter.

What James appears to have been trying to write was light, frothy, epigrammatic plays of the kind that Oscar Wilde was to make famous, but his condemnation of *A Woman of No Importance* as a "piece of helpless puerility" showed his failure to appreciate the kind of amiable unreality that was needed for this genre. The result was comedy that was not only grotesque but oddly inhuman. A critic at a New York performance of *Disengaged* for a hospital benefit described it as "nerveless, heartless, soulless."

The term "heartless" brings up a more serious matter. It has always struck me that James had a flaw of social conservatism, amounting at times to snobbishness, in his otherwise excellent sense of values. This is rarely apparent in his greater works. But in the novel that is most like a play, *The Awkward Age*, being made up almost entirely of dialogue, the lovely, lively heroine Nanda is rejected by the man she adores because he deems her purity to have been tainted by her exposure to the racey talk in her mother's sophisticated salon. Yet this man, Val, is not in the least represented as a prig. On the contrary he appears to be someone of whom James approves, having a proper depreciation of the low moral tone of modern London society, though he is amiable enough to take part in it. There is a shrill, old-maidish note in the book that may be explained by James's need for richly descriptive prose, as opposed to dialogue, to work out the full details of the point of view of any character under consideration. Hugh Walpole has this to say about James's conversation in private life: "His elaborate intricate sentences . . . came from his sense that words were not enough for the things of the mind. That was why, after an infinity of elaboration, the thing that he wanted to say would sometimes emerge at last trivial and unimportant."

Did James's characters in *speaking*, in dialogue, have the same trouble, so that only when their uttered words were amplified and modified by the full richness of his descriptive passages was the true depth and humaneness of their natures revealed? If, for example, we could see inside Val as we do Strether, perhaps we should better understand his psychological hang-up over "purity" in women. And if we were limited in knowing Basil Ransom of *The Bostonians* to what he actually says, we might regard him as a hopeless philistine. But when we can balance his denunciations of the "damnable femininization" of the world with his brooding memories of the terrible war in which he and his fellow Southerners had fought so long and so vainly, he becomes a much more sympathetic character.

Similarly, when Guy Domville proclaims with gloomy pride, "I'm the last of the Domvilles!," he seems to be affirming a somewhat trivial faith in ancestry, perhaps shared by his creator. We may even be tempted to exclaim, as did a heckling first-nighter: "And a damned good thing you are!" Yet the beautiful passage in *The Golden Bowl* likening Prince Amerigo's "dark blue eyes" to "the high windows of a Roman palace, of an historic front by one of the great old designers, thrown open on a feast day to the golden air" could give offense only to the most die-hard scorner of ancient dynasties. James had learned at last, in his "major" phase, not to rely on dialogue alone.

As a final comment on how little he had learned from the wasted theatre years, imagine asking an actress to deliver the following bit of exposition from the play version of *The Other House*, written a decade and a half after them:

Rose: Perhaps you know then that her detestable step-mother was, very little to my credit, my aunt. If her father, that is, was Mrs. Griffin's second husband, my uncle, my mother's brother, had been the first. Julia lost her mother. I lost both my mother and my father. It was then that Mrs. Griffen took me on; she had shortly before made her second marriage. She put me at the horrid school at Weymouth at which she had already put her stepdaughter. But it's the only good turn she has ever done us.

Tamburlaine

Existentialist Hero

The physical world evoked in the drama of Christopher Marlowe is certainly a beautiful and splendid one. It can boast of airy mountaintops and deep entrenched lakes whose banks are set with groves of fruitful vines. It is replete with glittering palaces and gilded tombs, with sumptuous temples studded with sundry colored stones and roofed aloft with curious work in gold. And its people, too, are lovely to look upon, majestic, muscular warriors and ladies fairer than the evening air clad in the beauty of a thousand stars. But the enchantment so created by Marlowe's vivid verse is not enhanced by the unlovely characters of even the loveliest people who inhabit this world; it is like a gallery of glorious art thronged with men and women who look not at the walls but only inwardly at their own shriveled souls.

For Marlowe's stage people have as little human sympathy for each other as he has for them. Barabas, the Jew of Malta, adores the "infinite riches" that he has amassed in a "little room," but his keenest zest is in the indulgence of his sadism by poisoning wells and killing disabled persons he comes across on dark nights. The weakling king, Edward II, of the eponymous play, almost bankrupts his kingdom to satisfy the greed of his minions, but the queen and the barons who rise at last to slay him are equally cruel and vindictive in their revenge. And the scholar Faustus, after selling his soul to gain infinite knowledge and power, tires of the secrets of the universe before his stipulated twenty-four years are up and wastes the balance of them playing crude practical jokes on the dupes his devil summons.

Only one character in all of Marlowe's drama seems to have won the author's admiration. He appears at moments of strenuous imagination to identify himself with Tamburlaine. It is Marlowe as well as the Tatar conqueror who dreams how passing brave it is "to be a king and ride in triumph through Persepolis." He never minimizes the utter brutality of his hero, but Tamburlaine is not a fool like Faustus, or an ass like Edward, or a freak like Barabas. He has the stature and splendor of Milton's Lucifer.

Jean Paul Sartre, in "L'Existensialisme est un Humanisme," makes the principal point that the new philosophy reverses the old order of "existence" and "essence." Essence, the concept of a man, had once been deemed to precede existence, his actual being. But Sartre reverses the order, putting existence first, so that each man is endowed from the start with the power to choose what he intends to be. And there is no god to help him or to judge him, no afterlife in which he may be rewarded or punished. A man is no more than the sum of his acts on earth. He cannot blame any but himself for what he becomes, because it is his own acts that have made him. Cowards and heroes are not born; they are created by cowardly or heroic acts. The determinist who holds his birth and environment responsible for his doings is a man of bad faith. Sartre calls his philosophy a humanism because it grants to each man a total liberty of action.

But there's a catch. When a man decides on a course of action, he decides it for all men. To see what his program really is he must see what the world would become if it was everyman's program. This is what Sartre calls *angoisse* (anguish), and that each man's decision must be made by him alone he calls *délaissement* (destitution).

When Tamburlaine captures the caravan of his wife-to-be, the divine Zenocrate, at the beginning of the first of the two plays devoted to his sanguinary career, he announces straight off his existentialist position:

> I am a lord, for so my deeds shall prove:
> And yet a shepherd by my parentage.
> But, Lady, this fair face and heavenly hue
> Must grace his bed that conquers Asia,
> And means to be a terror to the world,
> Measuring the limits of his empery
> By east and west as Phoebus doth his course.

To achieve his world aim he is absolutely and consistently ruthless. The white of his tents surrounding a besieged town will warn the inhabitants that surrender may still save their lives; when the tents are draped in black the entire population, if captured, will be put to the sword. In all of his conquests there is only a single act of mercy: he spares the life of Zenocrate's father. But he is not a dispassionate killer like Napoleon, limiting his slaughter to military necessity; he positively revels in blood.

> So shall our swords, our lances and our shot
> Fill all the air with fiery meteors:
> That when the sky shall wax as red as blood
> It shall be said I made it red myself,
> To make me think of nought but blood and war.

I suppose it could be argued that he uses terror to cow his opponents into quick surrender and save lives, but he never uses this as an argument. On the contrary he takes an actual glee in his atrocities, harnessing kings to his chariot and lashing their backs, putting them in cages, ordering his horsemen to trample to death the hapless virgins of Damascus, slaying with his own hand a son who has shirked his battle station. Tamburlaine appears to believe that bloodthirstiness is an essential part of the role he has chosen of Scourge of God.

The first play ends with the marriage of Tamburlaine and Zenocrate. All is still brilliant color and triumph in the resounding verse. Even the slaughtered dead are evoked to witness the glory of their conqueror.

> Millions of souls sit on the banks of Styx
> Waiting the black return of Charon's boat;
> Hell and Elysium swarm with ghosts of men
> That I have sent from sundry foughten fields,
> To spread my name through hell and up to Heaven.

Tamburlaine: Existentialist Hero

But in the second play we shall see that Tamburlaine has indeed been made by his own deeds. All men *have* acted as he has acted, and the world has become a mountain of skulls. The hero continues to triumph over everything but death, which at last takes first his beloved Zenocrate and finally himself. The stage seems to darken as we weary of the endless conquests and endless slaughter of the enemy. Even the verse seems to lose its luster. On the capture of Babylon the faithful Techelles asks Tamburlaine what is to be done with the wives and children. He should have known the answer.

Tamburlaine: Techelles, drown them all, man, woman and child. Leave not a Babylonian in the town.
Techelles: I will about it straight. Come, soldiers.

Tamburlaine himself degenerates now into a petty tyrant who kills the priests and burns the sacred books of Mohamet to prove to his troups that Allah is powerless to avenge the insult to his godhead and who razes the town that had the misfortune to be the death site of Zenocrate. But nothing can induce in him the smallest repentance for all his crimes against humanity. He is consistent to the end, as witnessed by his dying request.

Give me a map; then let me see how much
Is left for me to conquer all the world,
That these my boys may finish all my wants.

In a splendid production of the play with Anthony Quinn in the title role, servants hastened to unroll over much of the stage a vast carpet map of the world over which the expiring tyrant stomped in his death throes. If Marlowe really believed that there was no true glory on earth but the aspiration to power over one's fellow men, at least he had a clear vision of where it led. In our century he could have had his pick of Tamburlaines.

Three "Perfect Novels"
And What They Have in Common

I have classified *The Scarlet Letter*, *Wuthering Heights*, and *The Great Gatsby* as "perfect" for a special reason. In each case the author has created something totally unreal, yet at the same time totally satisfying, a dazzling artifact, compact, cohesive, a fine hard jewel that can be turned round and round, and admired from every angle. In each case the author has stripped himself, or herself, of the aids on which a reader normally relies to relate the page before him to some familiar aspect of his own environment. The author has deliberately chosen to be exotic. We see the conjurer, the magician at work.

A woman punished for life for a single fault, a monster of inhumanity on the Yorkshire moors, a bootlegger who lives in a fantasy world—the creators of such protago-

Address delivered at the Pierpont Morgan Library, New York, January 15, 1981. First appeared in limited edition pamphlet, Bruccoli Clark, Bloomfield Hills, Michigan, and Columbia, South Carolina, 1981.

nists cannot rely on their readers' recognition or identification. They are dealing almost with myths.

Now just what do I mean by that? I mean that they are dealing with human stories which, with the use of a little imagination, can be made to relate to any time or condition of man. We can be thrilled by these stories without ever wholly understanding them. Are myths ever meant to be wholly understood? Like Delphic oracles, they invite each man's interpretation. They have something to say to everybody.

THE SCARLET LETTER

Two of my chosen novels were published almost at the same time: *Wuthering Heights* in 1847 and *The Scarlet Letter* in 1850, and I start with the latter because it is set in an earlier era: that of the Massachusetts Bay Colony in the 1640s. The very name evokes the grim faces of Puritans in black cloaks with white ruff collars and condemning eyes, and there is nothing in *The Scarlet Letter* to contradict this impression.

I suppose the first thing that strikes a modern reader is that Hester Prynne would not be considered much of a sinner today. Consider her story. As a girl she is married off to a rich old man who is actually deformed. She is taken to a bleak new world, where her husband is captured by Indians, and she is left to her own devices in a colony where she has neither relatives nor friends. A beautiful young preacher, as silver-tongued as he is spiritual, falls in love with her, and she with him, and a child is born of their indiscreet passion. Did Hawthorne consider that so great a sin? One wonders. He is careful to make the point that if it was a sin, it nonetheless created an immortal soul.

It is certain, anyway, that he considered Hester's punishment of permanent ostracism as excessive. Well, then, we may ask, if neither the reader nor the author is supposed to consider the heroine as so dire a sinner, what is the book about? Injustice? No. There is no attempt to castigate the colonists. Hawthorne seems to accept their grim morality. He even seems at times almost to envy it. There is a distinct nostalgia in the way he harks back to a moral era of blacks and whites. I believe that he liked it as an artist, because it provided him with just the right case history in which to study what fascinated him most in human nature: the sense of sin.

The diary of Governor Winthrop, who, as a character, dies during the action of the novel and whose shroud is woven by the heroine, records the actual execution of a couple for adultery. The passage may well have given Hawthorne the seed of his novel:

At this court of assistants one James Britton, a man ill affected both to our church discipline and civil government, and one Mary Latham, a young woman about 18 years of age, whose father was a godly man and brought her up well, were condemned to die for adultery, upon a law formerly made and published in print. It was thus occasioned and discovered. This woman being rejected by a young man whom she had an affection unto, vowed she would marry the next man that came to her, and accordingly, against her friends' minds, she matched with an ancient man who had neither honesty nor ability, and one whom she had no affection unto; whereupon soon after she was married, divers young men solicited her chastity, and drawing her into bad company, and giving her wine and other gifts, easily prevailed with her, and among others this Britton, but God smiting him with a dread palsy and fearful horror of conscience withal, he could not keep secret, but discovered this.

The woman proved very penitent and had deep apprehension of the foulness of her sin. The man was very much cast down for his sins but was loth to die and petitioned for his life, but they would not grant it, though some of the magistrates questioned whether adultery was death by God's law. They were both executed; and died very penitently, especially the woman who had some comfortable hope of pardon of her sin, and gave good exhortation to all young maids to be obedient to their parents and to take heed of evil company.

One wonders why the Puritans made such a fuss about this crime that, like everything else, was preordained. For according to their grim theology, a man was saved or doomed irrevocably at birth. A lifetime of good works could not redeem the damned, nor could a lifetime of crime forfeit the reward of the blessed. They did, however, deem it at least possible to recognize the saved in this world by their discreet conduct and chastity, so there was always the hope, I suppose, that if you *looked* pious enough, you might fool God into thinking he had saved you. But this hope, if it existed, could not be acknowledged. It was the direst heresy. If God had damned you, he knew it, and there was nothing you could do about it.

So why, then, torture or hang the poor adulterers? Wouldn't eternal torment be enough for them? No. For even an adulterer *might* have been irrevocably elected for salvation by a quixotic deity, so at least you could give him a good licking on this earth.

Hawthorne found in the stern judges and conscience-stricken adulterers of New England the perfect laboratory in which to study guilt. Sin and guilt were almost synonymous in the Bay Colony; they fused to form the darkness in the heart of man. It did not so much matter what Hester had actually done, or whether the Puritans were right or wrong in condemning her, or even whether the faith of the colonists was valid or their religion true. What Hawthorne is depicting is a human soul alone, isolated from the crowd by an act deemed foul and shameful by the community and hence by the sinner. Hester accepts her shame not so much as a judgment as a fact. It is hers; it is *she*, and she must live with it, for it has made her. It is this existentialist element in the drama that makes it so close to us today.

For, as I have said, a myth speaks to any era, and so does this one. At least until the improbable day comes when man shall have ceased to have any guilt feelings at all. I find *The Scarlet Letter* an intenser statement of the agony of guilt than *Crime and Punishment*, perhaps precisely because the degree of the crime is in question. When I was a new boy in boarding school and was hazed, I felt, being a believer in the establishment, that even if I didn't know what I was being hazed for, I probably deserved it. Hester almost escapes her scarlet letter.

She learns the freedom of new thought and to look down on her bigoted persecutors. But she cannot in the end get away from her condition. She picks up the woven scarlet letter that she has cast off in the woods and silently puts it back on her bosom.

WUTHERING HEIGHTS

There is very little sense of guilt in *Wuthering Heights*, which may be what has led to a good deal of the tosh that is talked about Emily Brontë as an exponent of the "free soul." People like to imagine her stalking the moors in foul weather, her face set resolutely against the wind and rain. The noble profile in the National Portrait Gallery, which is probably of her sister Anne, is resolutely claimed for her by admirers. She is touted as a kind of mystic, indifferent to the demands of this world, eager to die and blend herself with the universe. She is likened to her character Heathcliff, who has been so romanticized that the Byronic hero enacted by Laurence Olivier was perfectly acceptable to the movie public.

In fact, Emily Brontë was not unlike her sisters. She cared very much about being published and was bitterly disappointed at the bad reviews of her only novel. She was perfectly capable of writing with the conventional prosiness of the era, as the opening chapters of *Wuthering Heights* demonstrate, so much so that E. F. Benson, a pusher of the "mystic" theory, was obliged to deduce that her brother Branwell had penned these pages, even though this explanation turned his "mystic" into a plagiarist. And she enjoyed good health until just before she died, and at the end she wanted very much to live. What then, was she trying to do in *Wuthering Heights*?

It is certainly a strange book. Its protagonist, Heathcliff, is so atrocious a character as to seem almost inhuman. Indeed the other characters constantly question the fact that he *is* human. He ruins the Earnshaw family and reduces the son, Hareton, who has never in the least harmed him, to poverty and illiteracy. He drives his poor wife, Isabella Linton, from his house by his brutalities. Some readers may think he is redeemed by his love for Catherine Earnshaw, but this love is totally selfish. After she has married Edgar Linton, he wants her to be wholly miserable, and indeed he makes her so, and when this misery results in her illness and death, he savagely maltreats and robs her only child. What was the point of writing the story of such a brute or madman?

The answer is that Heathcliff, like the white whale in *Moby-Dick*, can be pretty much anything the reader wants him to be: a devil or *the* devil, or the evil in man, or even the genius of man, or simply an old-fashioned villain. He is a force, which combined with a kindred force in Cathy, can sweep their world to destruction, but which, severed from it, will ultimately wither and perish. The novel is a series of combinations and confrontations: Heathcliff and old Mr. Earnshaw against the Earnshaws; Heathcliff and Cathy against Hindley Earnshaw; Cathy and Edgar Linton against Heathcliff and Isabella; Heathcliff and Cathy against the world; Heathcliff and his son against young Cathy and Edgar; and finally, Heathcliff alone against a united world.

Lord David Cecil sees the novel very aptly in terms of the struggle between Wuthering Heights and Thrushcross

Grange, the former representing all that is wild and rough and elemental in the countryside, and the latter all that is trim and ordered and neat. It is darkness against light; tempest against calm; war against peace. It is almost more of a symphony than a novel; it thrills the reader with its concussions and lulls him in its softer moments. He feels in touch with something elemental in life. Even if he's not quite sure what it is, there is a sense of catharsis. I suppose that is great art.

THE GREAT GATSBY

In *The Great Gatsby* Scott Fitzgerald makes a hero out of a kind of monster. Jay Gatsby, born James Gatz, acquires a fortune, or at least what appears to be one, by the age of thirty, by means that are far from clear but that are certainly dishonest. He starts with bootlegging, but in the end he seems to be engaged in the theft or embezzlement of securities. As Henry James leaves to our imagination how his heroes made their money (because he did not really know), so Fitzgerald allows us to make up our own crimes for Gatsby. But there is no doubt that he is a crook and a tough one, too. He has no friends, only hangers-on, no intellectual interests, no real concern for people. His entire heart and imagination are utterly consumed with his romantic image of Daisy Buchanan, a selfish, silly, giddy creature, who turns in the end into a remorseless hit-and-run driver. What seems to attract him to Daisy is the sense of financial security that she emanates: she has always been, and somehow always will be, abundantly, aboundingly rich. She is the tinselly department store window at Christmastime to the urchin in the street. Her very voice, as Gatsby puts it, "is full of money."

Fitzgerald is a courageous author. For what is Daisy, dreadful Daisy, but his dream and the American dream at that? He seems to make no bones about it. Vapid, vain, heartless, self-absorbed, she is still able to dispel a charm the effect of which on Gatsby is simply to transform him into a romantic hero. The American dream, then, is an illusion? Certainly. It is all gush and tinkle. But nonetheless its effect on a sentient observer is about all life has to offer.

Is Fitzgerald then seriously telling us that to fall in love with a beautiful heiress with a monied laugh, even if she's superficial, selfish, and gutless, is a fitting goal for a man's life, and one to justify years of criminal activity? Perhaps not quite. What he may be telling us is that he, the author, by creating the illusion of that illusion, may be doing the only thing worth doing in this vale of constant disillusionment.

To create his illusion of illusion Fitzgerald must set down the dismal atmosphere of Gatsby's life: the senseless, drunken parties, the dull, hard people, the inane conversations, the curious juxtaposition of the luxury of West Egg with the huge garbage dumps of Flushing— and yet make the whole gleam with a hard brittle beauty. It is difficult to see just how he does it, but he does. It is a book of beautiful sentences. Consider this passage in the epilogue:

> Most of the big shore places were closed now and there
> were hardly any lights except the shadowy, moving glow

of a ferryboat across the Sound. And as the moon rose higher the inessential houses began to melt away until gradually I became aware of the old island here that flowered once for Dutch sailors' eyes—a fresh, green breast of the new world. Its vanished trees, the trees that had made way for Gatsby's house, had once pandered in whispers to the last and greatest of all human dreams; for a transitory enchanted moment man must have held his breath in the presence of this continent, compelled into an aesthetic contemplation he neither understood nor desired, face to face for the last time in history with something commensurate to his capacity for wonder.

To me there is much in common between Fitzgerald's prose and the paintings of Edward Hopper. Hopper selects dull houses, drab streets, plain people, and invests them with a glow that is actually romantic. No matter what we think of Jay Gatsby and the triviality of his dream, it is impossible not to see what he sees and even feel a bit what he feels. I find myself almost embarrassed, in the end of the book, at regretting his sorry death. As one character says, "He had it coming to him." He certainly did. But Fitzgerald has caught the magic as well as the folly of Gatsby's dream.

There is a peculiar power in these three novels that may stem from the isolation of their protagonists. Hester lives in a world that is consistently cruel to her. Even those who care about her treat her harshly: her husband tortures her; her lover allows her to be punished alone. Heathcliff lives in a world that hates him and that he despises. Gatsby lives in a world where nobody understands him, except, in the very end, the narrator. Yet Nick Carraway's ultimate understanding of his friend costs him his own romance with Jordan Baker. He perceives at last that with *her* he does not even have the short-lived hope that Gatsby had of sharing with Daisy a perfect life.

The reader's experience with these three lonely characters is itself a lonely one. It is difficult to say just why one's reaction is so intense. Sometimes I think it is only self-pity. One likes to identify with a person as unjustly treated as Hester; it makes one feel the single sensitive soul in a world of horrid gaolers, and hence something finer than the world. One likes to identify with a dreamer like Gatsby whose dreams are better than anyone else's. Or even with Heathcliff, who revenges himself on a world that has mistreated him and then throws that world away. But the term "self-pity" may be simply denigrating. The business of living is a lonely one for all of us, and these novels repeat, embellish, and illuminate our own inner feelings.